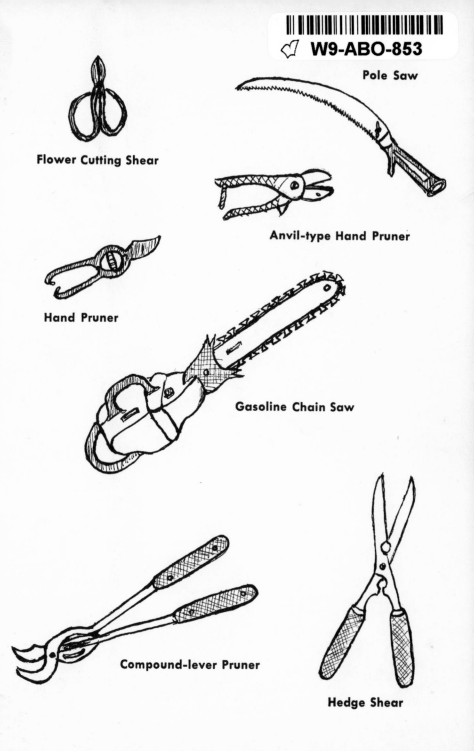

Flower Cutting Shear

Pole Saw

Anvil-type Hand Pruner

Hand Pruner

Gasoline Chain Saw

Compound-lever Pruner

Hedge Shear

THE
PRUNING
MANUAL

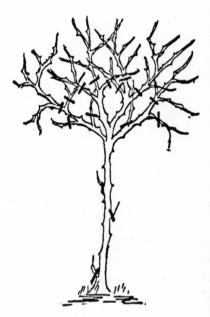

BY EDWIN F. STEFFEK
Illustrations by the Author

VAN NOSTRAND REINHOLD COMPANY
New York Cincinnati Toronto London Melbourne

Van Nostrand Reinhold Company Regional Offices:
Cincinnati, New York, Chicago, Millbrae, Dallas

Van Nostrand Reinhold Company Foreign Offices:
London, Toronto, Melbourne

Portions of this book were published under the title
Pruning Made Easy, by Henry Holt, New York, 1958.

Published by Van Nostrand Reinhold Company
450 West 33rd Street, New York, N.Y. 10001

Published simultaneously in Canada by
D. Van Nostrand Company (Canada), Ltd.

Contents

The Tree:

1. Terminals
2. Double leader (weak crotch)
3. Hangers or droopers (slow growers)
4. Branch stub
5. Weak crotch (narrow angle)
6. Strong crotch (wide angle)
7. Laterals from primary and secondary branches
8. Fruiting spurs
9. Water sprouts
10. Scaffold or main structural branch
11. Injuries from child's swing cables
12. Healing wound from properly cut branch
13. Trunk
14. Base of trunk
15. Base sucker
16. Root sucker
17. Lateral root
18. Tap root
19. Girdling root that will choke tree
20. Root improperly cut at curb laying
21. Feeder roots

PINE TIP

22. Main terminal shoot
23. Lateral branch, terminal removed
24. Laterals cut back
25. Lateral, terminal intact
26. One-year growth

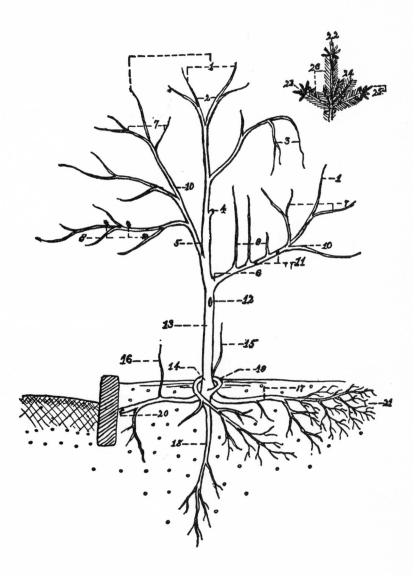

I. Why We Prune

If you were to ask ten different people why they prune, you might get as many as ten different answers, all sincere and all correct. The reason, as you have probably guessed, is that each one has a different purpose, a different aim or end to be gained.

You have probably also witnessed several techniques, including those of the "barber" who gives everything a crew cut with a pair of hedge shears, the "butcher" who sails into his plants and cuts everything in sight down to the bare bones, and the "timid soul" who hasn't the heart to cut anything—to cut out a branch hurts him almost as much as to cut off his arm.

In view of all these uncertainties this book purposes to guide you into approaching pruning sensibly and intelligently; to show you how, why, and when to prune in order to meet your particular objective.

WHAT IS PRUNING?

Before we get into *how* to prune or even the *why*, we have to know exactly what pruning *is*. Pruning is the art of cutting or otherwise removing unwanted plant growth to make the plant grow or behave the way you want it to as distinguished from shearing or "haircutting." Pruning is simple, when you approach it sensibly and intelligently and know just what you want to accomplish.

Climate may enter into it, but only to a certain extent. There are no general rules. In some cases you may prune severely in cold climates because of freezing back. Yet, in warm climates you may prune to an equal extent—because the favorable growing conditions have produced an excessive amount of growth. The only conclusion you can safely draw is that climate does govern your timing, the same as other local conditions, such as elevation exposure, and the vagaries of the season.

We may ask, Why don't we let nature be our guide? But Mother Nature's purposes are not always the same as ours. Nature does not care how many long-stemmed, fully double roses we get, or that our apples be big, unblemished, and rosy cheeked. All she cares about is that each plant survive and produce its seed to cover the bare earth with its kind. Everything else is secondary: the dying off and loss of the lower branches on pines to produce clear, knot-free lumber; the thinning out of branches in a tree top to reduce obstruction to the wind and lessen the danger of blowing down; and so on.

Nature runs no production line; no two plants are exactly the same. Consequently, pruning is largely a matter of common sense, of judgment, once you have learned the guiding principles and decided exactly what you want to accomplish. This book aims merely to put the tools into your hands, so to say—to outline these principles, to show you what to do and why. The rest is up to you!

And now, what are the basic reasons for pruning? There are nine.

1. *To Train Plants into Desired Forms*

Apples are easier to pick if the tree branches are low and all parts can be reached conveniently from a not-too-tall ladder. The common forsythia is considered graceful if it bends to the ground in a sweeping reverse curve. A privet hedge best serves its purpose when it is trimmed severely, and stands stiff and erect like a living green wall. A maple should look like a gigantic lollipop, with no erring branches to mar its symmetrical form. A wisteria should drop its flowers in festoons over the entire length of its trellis. Boston ivy should be kept from sprawling its octopus-like way across the roof. All these and many others are reasons for pruning not to please nature, but to make the plants conform to our ideas of what is most useful, convenient, or beautiful.

2. *To Rejuvenate Old Plants*

When a small tree or shrub grows old and increasingly unproductive of new growth, flowers, or fruit, we often cut it back. A lilac that has seen its best days may be cut off almost to the ground, a third of the plant each year for three years, and vigorous new stems encouraged to take the place of the tired old stems. This sort of rejuvenation we see again in the annual cutting to the ground of the blackberry and raspberry canes that have just fruited.

3. To Increase Flowering and Fruiting

Hand in hand with injecting new life into old plants goes pruning to increase production of flowers and fruit. Sometimes it is an old plant and sometimes it is a young one, but the end is the same: to get more out of it. If a tree is producing too-long stem growth at the expense of blossoms, we head it back. That is, we cut off part of it to force out more side branches and, we hope, fruiting buds.

If branches are too close together so that one shades another, flowers and fruit do not form properly. We cut off the offending branches. If a branch is so twiggy that it is all leaf and stem growth, flowers and fruits have a bad time. We then thin the twigs or cut off the offending portion and let a strong new growth take over.

4. To Decrease the Amount of Fruit

Just the opposite can happen. Sometimes a tree or shrub tries to bear so much fruit or so many blossoms that it would be seriously weakened. At other times no harm would come to the plant but now the competition is so severe that there just isn't enough food to nourish all the clamoring fruits. The tree would either be forced to shed some—and usually too many (in plums, for instance, we sometimes call this June drop)—or none of them would amount to much. If this is so, we either remove some of the small branches or, usually, just the fruits themselves. We call this thinning but it is just another form of pruning.

5. To Open Up for Better Ripening

Sometimes a tree grows too thick, especially where we have headed it back to keep it from getting too tall. Sun cannot get into the tree to ripen the fruit sufficiently. Of course, this is more important to the commercial grower, who must have attractively colored fruits, than to the home gardener. But even he likes handsome, rosy-cheeked fruits for he knows that they contain more sugar, hence are sweeter and more flavorsome.

Here the gardener must thin out to let the sun in, especially when he had headed in the leading shoots to keep the branches within reach. We used to do this a great deal on tomatoes as well, but the practice has died out somewhat, for we now know that tomatoes can ripen, even when picked green.

6. *To Prevent Future Damage*

If two branches or a trunk and a branch grow too close together so that the resulting crotch is very narrow, one must be removed. If not, the annual increase in thickness would not cement the two together but slowly wedge them apart until someday, during a high wind or under the weight of a heavy crop, one would split off. This is a common trouble with the old Abundance plum.

Sometimes one branch rubs against another. Here the protecting bark may be rubbed off and disease enter. It is better to remove one of the branches. Again, you may find a split branch. The only cure in most cases is to cut it off before it breaks farther and strips the bark off down the trunk as it goes.

7. *To Keep to Desired Size*

This, of course, applies to all kinds of trees and shrubs. As we mentioned before, apples are easier to pick, if the tree is kept low enough that all parts can be reached easily. It also makes spraying and all other operations simpler and therefore less expensive. It helps minimize danger of wind toppling in severe storms.

Trimming a hedge comes into the same category, that is, cutting to retain a desired size and shape. The same goes for standard or "tree" roses, heliotropes, and geraniums. And it is particularly important with dwarfs and the trained trees known as espaliers. Although they are grown on special roots to keep them small, they still need judicious trimming back from time to time to keep them exactly as intended.

8. *To Remove Injury and Disease*

If a branch breaks in a winter ice storm, what do you do? You cut it off. If a plum tree develops a cankerous growth, what do you do? You cut it off. It is as simple as that. Here is another and important reason for pruning—cutting off injured or diseased parts of the tree or shrub to prevent further damage.

9. *To Produce Special Forms*

We have already touched upon the training of hedges and the trimming of espaliers. This is pruning to create and maintain plants in special forms—candelabrum, vase, diamond pattern, and so on—especially for use against walls to produce a geometrical pattern as well as unusually fine fruits.

Training plants into dog shapes, cat shapes, columns, pyramids, and spirals is called topiary work. Unlike training espaliers, which are usually grown against a fence or wall and are two-dimensional, this entails producing the desired form in three dimensions. Topiary art is therefore the most extreme expression of pruning for 'form. A similar sort of severe pruning is of course used in the original production of the standards, or tree roses, etc.

To sum up, there are many kinds of pruning for many purposes, and how you prune depends to a very large extent upon what you are trying to do. All of them have one thing in common, however. They remove from a given plant some portion that interferes with *our* plans—our ideas of how the plant should look or behave, not nature's.

II. What Plants Are Like—and What Happens When We Prune

Before we describe *how* to prune, let us consider the physical make-up of plants so that the terms will not appear strange and you will understand *why* we do some things and not others.

WHAT STEMS ARE LIKE

If you look at the end of a branch cut off crosswise you will find there are different layers or rings. In the center is the pith, a soft spongy material that is of little importance to the pruner except in the few trees where it is unusually thick, as in the walnut group and the sumacs. In these, it is somewhat more important to protect the cut ends of branches with a dressing to prevent the entrance of decay into this soft core.

Around the pith is the heartwood, for practical purposes dead tissue that merely lends stiffness or mechanical support to help hold up the active parts of the tree. You must have noticed many times how a tree continues to live with the whole center rotted away. That is the reason. The center of the trunk or branch is no longer essential to its life processes.

Outside the heartwood is the sapwood. This carries on practically all the work of conducting water and salts upward within the tree. Usually it is lighter in color than the heartwood, an extreme case being the distinctly two-toned wood of the red cedar, and is made up primarily of organ-pipelike cells that serve as ducts.

Encircling the sapwood is a layer, usually microscopically thin, called the cambium. Here is where all growth occurs. On the inside the cambium lays down wood cells, while on the outside it produces those that eventually become the bark. Even though the cambium is so thin we cannot see it with the naked eye, it is the most important of all the tissues, for it is the seat of all life. If it is ever damaged completely, it can never be regenerated. That is why trees that have had their bark peeled off down to the wood quickly die. These cells must never be allowed to dry out. They are also easily killed by

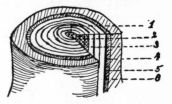

Typical broad-leaved branch or trunk: 1 pith, 2 heartwood, 3 sapwood showing annual rings (light spring, dark summer), 4 cambium, 5 inner bark or phloëm, 6 bark

such materials as tar oil, creosote, and turpentine and, if exposed, are readily attacked by disease organisms. The cambium is vitally important in another way, for in grafting these tissues must meet to make the unions effective.

Outside the cambium is what we generally refer to as the inner bark. Its proper name is phloëm (flo'-em). It is usually a fairly thin layer of bright green tissue. Its main job is to pass the food, usually in the form of sugar, manufactured in the leaves, back down to the roots and to feed the all-important cambium.

Thus, you can readily see why nothing must happen to this layer, either. If the supply line is broken by girdling or removing the bark around the tree, whether by man's activities or those of mice or insects, the tree must eventually die of starvation. It is also easy to see why a label wire left on a young tree can kill it, why supporting a branch is better done by putting a bolt through it rather than a cable around it, and why a swing or guy wire can cause permanent injury. But, we can also turn this girdling to our advantage. By cutting a ring around the twig we can increase the size and sugar content of grapes and assist the formation of roots by the concentration of sugars at this point in propagating by "air layering."

Outside all the tree's tissues is the bark, made up of old, worn-out, dead cells from the inner bark. The bark serves an important purpose. It acts as insulation against rapid changes in temperature, cuts down the loss of water from the inner tissues, and protects them from physical injury. Bark splits, checks, or scales off because, being dead, it cannot stretch to accommodate the expanding tissues beneath it; the particular pattern by which it does this is characteristic of the kind of tree or shrub.

HOW A STEM GROWS THICKER

Each year with the awakening of the plant in the spring or the coming of the rainy season, water, bearing minerals from the soil, surges upward through the sapwood to the leaves. Here it is converted into starches and then to sugars, after which it works its way downward in the inner bark to feed all the active parts of the tree.

This brings us to the subject of annual rings. In the spring when growth is rapid a layer of big coarse cells is produced. In summer when growth slows down, large water-carrying ducts are not needed. The new cells then are much smaller and consequently the wood is more compact. This results in two distinct rings: the large, light, coarse spring wood and the darker, tighter, harder summer wood. Thus, to determine the age of any such stem all we do is count the number of light or dark rings, one for each year.

WHAT A TWIG IS LIKE

Now that we know something of the interior make-up of stems and branches, let us turn to the outside. All growth in length comes from buds. These contain a spot of cambium called the growing point. At the tip of the main stem and the tip of every branch down to the smallest twig is one or more buds. These are called terminal buds and are responsible for the lengthening of the branches. Down along the twig are other buds, usually smaller, called lateral buds. These may be in clusters (whorls) of five, as in some of the pines; in pairs, one on each side of the twig, as in the maples, ashes, and lilacs; or arranged alternately as in roses. Usually these are found in the axils (the angle formed by leaf and stem) of the leaves or just above the leaf scar of the previous year's growth. These provide for new side branches. Normally, the greater growth comes from the terminal buds.

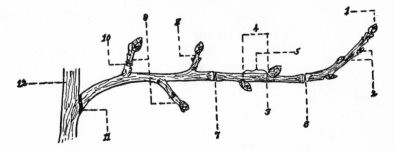

Twig (apple or pear): 1 *terminal bud,* 2 *lateral buds,* 3 *leaf scar,* 4 *nodes (joints),* 5 *internode,* 6 *annual rings (last year's growth from here out),* 7 *annual rings (previous growth, here to 6),* 8 *spur that has not yet fruited,* 9 *spurs that have fruited,* 10 *annual rings on spur,* 11 *annual rings (twig started growth from here),* 12 *parent branch*

When growth begins again after a dormant or rest period not all the formed buds grow, even though they are uninjured. These are dormant buds, held in reserve, ready to grow if something happens to the others.

Still farther down the twig may be buds in such rudimentary form that you may never see them. But let some catastrophe befall the others up above, such as the removal of the upper portion of the branch, and immediately these adventitious buds, as they are called, seem to come out of nowhere below the wound and produce long, new shoots.

There is still another way to classify buds—leaf buds and flower buds. By far the most plentiful are the first group. They are usually much more slender and pointed, their sole function being to produce new leaf and stem growth. The others are generally much fatter and fewer in number, their job being to produce flowers. Flower buds may be terminal, as in lilacs and Mayflowered viburnums, clustered along the stem with the leaf buds, as in the peach and flowering quinces, or on little pedestals called spurs, as in apples and pears. In any case, flower buds are always fatter than leaf buds.

The important point to remember is that the buds are not formed in spring, as most people believe, but toward the end of the previous growing season. This is usually in midsummer in four-season areas, and with the approach of the dry season in the wet-dry climates. Thus, any cutting when the buds are forming or have formed but not yet started growth has a decided effect on the leaf bud—flowered bud ratio of all flowering plants that bloom after their rest period.

One more subject we might touch upon here is why all buds do not grow at once. It is believed by some authorities that the buds on upper parts of the stem give off hormones that prevent the buds below them from sprouting. Then, when these buds or stem tips are pruned off the hormones no longer are present and the dormant or advantitious buds can grow.

WHAT HAPPENS WHEN YOU CUT

All that we have been discussing up to now about the stem structure and kinds of buds may sound purely academic but it isn't. All these things play an important part when you prune. For instance, you now know that new shoots can come only from buds and must contain some cambium. They cannot come from the heartwood of a stub or stump.

But, to get down to something still more practical, when a branch is cut off, what happens? Immediately the nearest buds take over and try to assume the position of those cut off. When you remove a terminal, the nearest side-shoot buds grow much more than they normally would and, barring accident, the nearest one becomes the new terminal. Thus, when we want to make a shoot

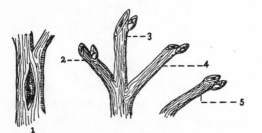

1 how to shape large wound to aid drainage, promote healing, 2 cut too far above bud, 3 too high, too sharp angle, 4 too close to bud, 5 cut properly

branch out, we cut off the tip and the branches come out at the sides.

The strength and vigor of the new shoot is often directly proportional to the amount we cut the stem back. For instance, if we prune a lilac or flowering quince back severely, to six or eight inches from the ground, there will be little stem growth to support. Hence, the new growth will have little competition for nutrients and will be strong and the flowers, if any, fewer. But if we cut only the tips off, all the earlier branches will still be there and the new growth will be smaller and weaker. The flowers will be more plentiful although smaller, since they must all compete for the same food. Thus, if you want many small fruits or a large number of small flowers for a mass effect in your garden, prune lightly. If you want fewer but high-quality blooms or fruits, prune severely to concentrate the strength in those few you want.

We can shape a plant by the location of the top bud that we leave. If it comes out from the right side of the twig, the new branch will grow to the right. If from the left, the branch will be to the left. Thus, if we want to close up a straggly shrub, we cut so that the topmost buds point inward. If we want to open up a tree or rose bush, we not only cut out some of the center growth but we select as top buds to leave those that point outward.

A tree or shrub with two stems of equal size and vigor competing for dominance can be guided by the length we cut them back. If we leave one appreciably taller than the other, it will eventually assume dominance over the other, the amount being in direct proportion to their difference in length after pruning.

HOW TO MAKE THE CUT

How the cut is made will determine to a large extent the future health of the tree. Suppose your cut leaves a stub projecting from the parent stem or beyond the last bud. What happens? At first, nothing. But the stub usually dies and stays there. Eventually rot sets in, works down the stub, and finally into the branch beneath it. Years later it has a weak, rotten center. The moral is, never leave a stub. Always cut as close to a bud as you can without injuring it or as close as possible to the parent stem so the new growth can quickly heal over the wound.

According to these points, it becomes important how you hold your shears. If you are using the scissor type—a blade cutting next to another blade or flattened branch holder—keep the cutting blade just as close to the parent stem as you can. If the shear is of the anvil type—a blade cutting against a bed of soft metal—the chances of a smooth cut will be even better but it will be doubly important to cut as near to the trunk as possible, since you can't get in as close with this type.

The next thing to watch is whether you cut from above or below the branch, unless the growth is so tight that there is only one way to get the shears in. Wherever possible, cut from the bottom up. In this way you avoid getting the blade wedged into a tight crotch.

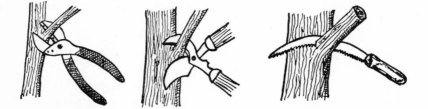

How to cut small or moderate branches: 1 cutting blade below to prevent binding, 2 again from below, 3 small cut made below first, main cut from above

On the other hand, if the branch is so large you must use a saw, cut from the top down. In this way the weight of the branch tends to keep the cut open and prevents the saw binding, as would easily happen were the cut made from below. Also, bearing down as you saw is much easier than pushing up. Before you make the cut, however, there is an important preliminary. Make a shallow cut through the bark on the underside to prevent stripping the bark down the parent stem if the branch cracks before the sawing is completed.

If the branch is a very heavy one, first saw off the end a foot or two beyond where you intend to make the final cut. This eliminates the weight problem and you can make your final cut at leisure and without danger of harming the tree.

In the case of branches over half an inch or so in diameter, it is also advisable to protect the wound from decay while it heals. Paint it with one of the commercial tree wound dressings. Lacking this, give it a coat of outside house paint. The protection is not as good but is better than none.

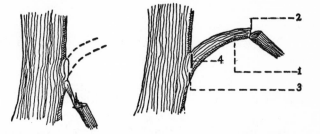

Left, *bark stripped by improper cutting*. Right, *correct way to cut:* 1 *protective cut below,* 2 *branch removed leaving generous stub,* 3 *protective cut beneath final one,* 4 *final cut made from above*

Where the branch removed was really large it often helps the wound's healing to cut the surrounding bark into a point, top and bottom, making a vertical ellipse before painting. This enables the cambium to roll back over the injury more easily from the sides and hastens healing.

III. The Tools for the Job

You can't do any job properly without the right tools. Pruning is no exception. If you are going to do any amount of it, buy the best tools you can find. Cheap ones not only do a poor job but are troublesome to the pruner. Try them before buying and be sure they are not only made of good steel but that the workmanship is of high quality.

HAND PRUNERS

Most useful of all and the first to buy are hand shears. These come in two basic types. The first and older sort is the drop-forged shears with a beveled blade that cuts down the side of a heavy hook or branch holder, much as a pair of scissors works. This is the type generally preferred by professionals for the good, close cut it makes. But the shears must be of good quality or the two parts will eventually spring out of shape and the branch will be wedged in between, becoming badly mangled. I have had this happen to me many times with cheap shears. It is most disconcerting to the pruner as well as harmful to the plant. A variant of this type of shears is one with two cutting blades. These are good tools but seldom seen in this country.

The other basic type is one in which the blade cuts down on a bed of soft metal. This is very easy to operate and is often preferred by the home gardener. It cuts slightly less close to the trunk or parent branch but in many cases this factor is less important than the ease of cutting.

Either type may come with a flat, coiled, or cylindrical spring. The difference is immaterial so long as it works well. One thing to insist on is an effective safety catch to keep the shears closed when not in use. Shears that pop open at the wrong time can be a nuisance. They can also be the cause of a serious accident.

Many professionals also like to use a pruning knife. This can have either a fixed blade or one that folds into the handle. Both types are good. The important thing is a sturdy hooked blade that will not slip off the branch being cut and thus be a hazard to pruner and plant alike. Also it needs to be fastened firmly into the handle so that small branches can be lopped off with one quick motion.

LONG-HANDLED PRUNERS

Sometimes called loppers, these are for cutting heavier branches. They vary from the single-jointed type that cuts branches up to an inch or an inch and a quarter in diameter, to compound pruners in which levers or a slot arrangement greatly multiply the force applied. The compound pruner enables the operator to cut branches of large size without making a cut from several sides, as would be necessary with single-jointed shears.

Besides selecting a good steel and a tool with a proper feeling of balance, ascertain that the handles are properly attached to stand the strain of cutting heavy branches. The simple type will often serve if long ferrules join the handle to the shear, but the compound types should have steel handles running the full length.

Hedge shears are sometimes also considered in this group but they cut only very small branches, usually even lighter ones than the hand pruners, unless equipped with a heavy-duty cutting notch at the base of one or both blades. Good solid handles are necessary here, too. Beware of hedge shears, however, for much undesirable "haircutting" of trees and shrubs is perpetrated with them in the name of pruning.

POLE PRUNERS

From the above we graduate to the various pole pruners that enable one to reach up and cut off branches eight to fifteen or more feet in the air. Though they rarely cut branches over an inch in diameter they are most useful. The two things to watch when buying are the length of pole and the compounding of the cutting force. Some have a rope fastened directly to a lever on the opposite end of the cutting blade. These are the least compounded and hence cut smaller branches than the others. Greater cutting power is achieved by a rod running to another arm that further compounds the cutting effort. The compounding is a big help, for cutting far over one's head is hard enough in any event.

On some pruners, this connecting rod runs the length of the pole to the operating handle below. This offers positive cutting power but it usually prevents the addition of added lengths of pole and thus limits the reach. When extensions are necessary it is much better to have the type in which the compounding or lower lever arm is placed high on the pole and a rope is attached to its tip. This gives maximum cutting power while permitting the use of extension poles.

HAND SAWS

For branches too large for shears the obvious recourse is to saws. Unlike ordinary carpenter's saws, which usually stick when cutting green wood, these are made with especially coarse, wide-set teeth. Thus, they not only bite deeply but make the cut wider than the blade of the saw, eliminating the danger of sticking.

If you are going to be guided by the professionals, tree surgeons usually prefer a broad saw, shaped much like a crosscut but with different teeth. Orchardists, on the other hand, lean toward small, pointed saws, shaped like a carpenter's compass or keyhole saw. The latter may be curved or straight. It maybe collapsible so that it folds into its own handle, have a fixed handle, or be such that it can be mounted on a long handle like a pole pruner. Whichever type you select, the important things to watch for are teeth that will take a good bite without clogging up with wet sawdust, and good steel—which "sings" if you tap it when bent.

POWER TOOLS

These are not needed for ordinary pruning but there are times when they can be useful.

First, there are the power chain saws. For large jobs the gasoline-driven chain saws are unsurpassed but because of their weight they are intended for ground use. Of lighter weight and generally somewhat less capacity, are the electric saws. They are not adaptable to use away from a power outlet but often they may be carried part way up into the tree. The saw that is best for you depends upon your needs.

Brush and small trees can be quickly removed with a circular saw mounted on the front of a garden tractor. This will cut a prodigious amount in a short time, if the land is such that you can wheel a hand tractor over it. These are gasoline-driven machines and run like any rotary lawn mower.

The power tool most frequently seen among home gardeners is probably the electric hedge shears. Simple and light, it operates somewhat like a miniature hay-mowing machine, with cutting teeth that operate against or between rake-like teeth that hold the stems in place for cutting. These shears are most useful for hedges and topiary work—cutting plants into fancy shapes—but should not be confused with the true pruners, which are adapted to selective cutting, removing some branches and leaving others instead of cutting everything.

WOUND DRESSINGS

While not tools, these are an important part of the pruner's equipment, for every cut stem one-half inch or more in diameter runs the risk of rot gaining entry before it heals over. Thus anything that prevents the entrance of decay does much to maintain the health of the tree or shrub.

A commercially prepared wound dressing obtainable at any good garden center or seed store is the best bet. However, there are some who prefer to mix their own, using raw linseed oil and Bordeaux powder. This is inexpensive and effective but the light blue shows on the tree much more than the black of the commerical preparations. When neither is available, a good linseed-oil outside house paint makes a fairly good substitute. Choose an inconspicuous color if you can.

FOR RELIABLE TOOLS

Since tools of good quality are necessary for good workmanship, it seems worth while to include a list of some of the makers whose names usually mean reliability. While there are still others deserving of such attention, these are the best known and those whose products you are most likely to see: Some make hand tools, some the larger sorts:

Acme Shear Co.
Bridgeport, Conn.

Bartlett Mfg. Co.
3003 East Grand Ave.
Detroit 2, Mich.

Coleman Tree Pruners
Tioga Center, N.Y.

Corona Clipper Co.
510 Ramona Ave.
Corona, Cal.

Henry Disston & Son, Inc.
Unruh & Milnor Sts.
Tacony, Phila. 35, Pa.

J. T. Henry Co.
Hamden, Conn.

Kaufman Mfg. Co.
29th & Meadow Lane
Manitowoc, Wis.

Porter-Cable Machine Co.
2770 N. Salmon St.
Syracuse 8, N.Y.

H. K. Porter, Inc.
74 Foley St.
Somerville, Mass.

Sargent & Co.
New Haven, Conn.

Seymour, Smith & Sons, Inc.
Oakville, Conn.

Stanley Tools
Div. of The Stanley Works
New Britain, Conn.

True Temper Corp.
Cleveland, Ohio

J. Wiss & Sons Co.
Newark 7, N.J.

IV. The Young Tree

There is an old saying to the effect that as the twig is bent, so will the sapling grow. With pruning the results are even more positive, for a bent twig can be straightened but a branch cut off can never be grown back on. So, more than ever, the way you start a young tree out in life determines how it will look and perform for all its many years to come. It matters not whether it is an ornamental or a fruiting tree.

WHEN THE TREE ARRIVES

Young trees may come in any of three ways. They may be delivered in roofing paper pots or large cans, a method used widely on the West Coast and less commonly over the rest of the country. They may be balled and burlapped or they may come bare-root, wrapped in moss, shavings, or similar material.

In any case, when the tree arrives it needs a thorough examination. The nurseryman has done his best to produce a shapely top and to fortify it with a good root system through periodic root pruning or transplanting. But even with the best of care tops can arrive broken, and roots, too, if shipped bare.

Damaged tops should be cut back at least to good, healthy wood and preferably to a bud pointing in the direction you want the new growth to take. Trees arriving otherwise than in cans will need still more severe cutting, as we shall see later.

Broken roots, especially, should be cut off back to good, healthy growth, for in the soil any injury that does not heal readily is exposed to the entry of decay bacteria. Thus it is of paramount importance that no jagged ends be left, although it is rarely necessary

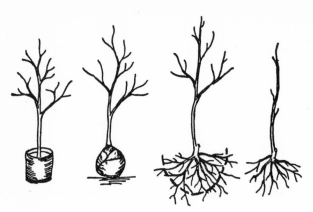

*Young trees as they come from the nursery (l to r): in can, balled
and burlapped, bare root showing where roots were cut in dig-
ging, one-year whip*

to paint the stubs. After inspection and trimming, if time and space
permit, it is often a good idea to soak bare roots overnight in a pail
of water. A little quick-acting fertilizer in the water at this time will
often help too, although it is not necessary.

THE BARE-ROOTED TREE

Now, let us return to top-pruning the bare-rooted tree, because
this is the hardest one of all to handle. Obviously, since these trees
have suffered the greatest root loss, the top must be cut back in a
correspondingly severe manner to restore the proper balance between roots and tops. A good rule to follow is that bare-rooted plants,
especially rapid-growing types, may have up to two-thirds of the
top removed. Thin, sparsely branching, or slower types may do
better with only one-third removed.

Some trees, such as apples and pears, especially those sold for
commercial use, are often sold as one-year whips, just a simple long
stem with no branches. With these the shaping of the tree must be
borne in mind at the outset. The whip is usually cut off just above
the point where the lowest branches are wanted. This induces buds
to appear and branches to develop at the top of the remaining
stem.

Most fruit and ornamental trees, however, are usually sold as two-year, three-year, or older specimens on which structural branches have already begun to develop. The remedial pruning can be handled in two ways. First, the top growth and all branches can be shortened equally, leaving the final selection of branches until the next pruning. A better way, in most cases, is to select the branches that will form the main framework of the tree, nipping back only their soft ends to prevent wilting and removing completely or almost completely all other branches.

Balled and Canned Specimens

A well-balled plant—not one with a bag of loose soil or one just dug—is better able to withstand transplanting. Hence, pruning is less severe. Shaping the tree is more important than cutting back to restore growth balance, although some of the latter must still be done.

The tree delivered in a five-gallon can, finally, suffers almost no setback if the can is cut and removed without disturbing the soil. Here, the pruning may be confined almost entirely to guiding the tree into the proper form.

THE SECOND PRUNING

In most cases, this is the most important single pruning in the life of the tree, for it is now that the basic structural branches are selected and its usefulness as a tree all its life decided.

A healthy and vigorous tree, planted properly in good soil, should respond to its first pruning with strong new growth both above and below ground. If no shaping is done the first year, it is doubly important for the main framework of the tree to be started in the second year.

Except for a little nipping off of soft tips and rubbing off of unwanted buds, pruning is usually done when the tree is dormant, not growing. In warmer climates it can often be done any time after growth ceases; in the colder states it is usually done in winter or very early spring. Where there is any danger whatsoever of twigs or branches freezing back, such as with peaches in the North, pruning is done only before growth starts in spring.

Now for the actual pruning. First, remove any unwanted

branches. Then, if a wide, open tree is desired, leave the terminal or end buds untouched on all the remaining branches and remove their stronger-growing laterals. This system, however, is rarely used because it produces an open, weaker-branched tree. Its greatest usefulness is with trees that tend to produce too many branches, hence become too tight.

Young fruit tree showing first three year's pruning

Generally, a compact, sturdy tree is preferred. It is better able to carry its load, if a fruit tree, and better able to withstand the buffeting of storm winds. Here the terminal buds on the desired branches are removed along with a quarter to a third of the new growth to encourage secondary branching.

Unless it is necessary to force out structural branches, the main terminal shoot of the tree is cut back little, if at all. However, a tall, leggy tree is not usually desirable, and serious thought should be given this point at all times. Neither should competition for the leader be tolerated. A multiheaded tree is easily broken. Too-low branches should be avoided, as future troublemakers. Remove them any year as soon as there are others coming out of the trunk at the desired height.

FURTHER PRUNING

By the third and fourth years the dominant position of the leader should be well established and more attention can now be paid to producing the tree's final shape. Branches should be encouraged to throw out secondary and tertiary branching and the tree's leader kept from making runaway growth. Watch for branches that are growing too close together and would later fight branches growing directly under and shaded by others, damaged or broken branches, and branches that bend down or otherwise get in the way.

ADDITIONAL POINTS TO BEAR IN MIND

(1) Trees grow at the tips. They do not stretch like a rubber band. A branch that starts out from the trunk at the height of five feet will always be at this height. It will never be pulled higher.

(2) A little corrective pruning or rubbing off of unwanted buds during the growing season will save much work during the dormant season and cause much less shock to the tree than an amputation later.

(3) Generally, fruit trees should be branched as low as working around them permits. Picking, spraying, and pruning will be easier. Ornamentals, on the other hand, should be headed higher since they are more likely to be subject to traffic under them or to have smaller plants, like shrubs, around them.

(4) Trees from the warmer, wetter parts of the world may tend to grow shorter and more dumpy. Train them upward by removing the bottommost branches and thinning out above. If necessary, feed and water a little more than usual. This will turn them into more attractive trees.

V. What to Do with Shrubs

In this chapter we shall deal with the large group of deciduous shrubs—those that drop their leaves with the approach of cold weather—which make up the bulk of permanent plantings in colder areas.

The pruning of shrubs is much like that of young trees. When we cut off a branch the remaining buds respond the same way. We open up the branching the same way and we tighten it up the same way. There is one important difference, however. Trees are usually trained to a single trunk, with branching only above a certain point. Shrubs are usually trained to throw up several stems and to start branching from the ground up.

AT PLANTING TIME

Like trees, shrubs arrive from the nursery in cans, balled, or bare-root. Damaged or broken stems and roots are removed with a clean cut to promote healing. The tops of bare-root plants are cut back one-third or more to compensate for the loss of roots. The main thing to keep in mind is that single-stemmed or high-branching shrubs are undesirable, so we prune shrubs to branch from the ground up. If necessary to induce branching, cut the stems back even as low as six inches or less from the ground, always cutting down to an outward-facing bud unless the shrub is scraggly and needs to be tightened.

TIME TO PRUNE

When to prune an established flowering shrub is often a big question in the minds of new gardeners. A good rule is, those that bloom in spring on wood of the previous year's growth are pruned in late spring or early summer—that is, immediately after blooming is over so they can throw out new growth and buds for next year's bloom. Those that bloom later, on growth of the current year, are generally pruned in late winter or early spring before growth starts but late enough to eliminate any portions injured during cold weather. However, if you are one who finds it difficult to remember when to prune, a fairly safe practice is to prune any shrub right after flowering is over.

Left, *how to prune after planting.* Right, *one year later*

In the Far West and South, where only partial dormacy may take place, newly transplanted Easterners or Northerners often make one serious mistake—they cut back their shrubs severely during the short winter. The return of plant food from leaf and stem to the roots is often not yet completed and the plant suffers a serious shock from this deprivation. These gardeners, instead, should wait until growth is about to start, or cut moderately and spread the rejuvenation over several years. This is especially important with such plants as leonotis and buddleia. The end of the dormant period is also the time to cut back to the ground such plants as red-stemmed dogwoods and those willows that are grown only for their color-fully stemmed new growths.

TO MAINTAIN SHAPE

Established shrubs often lose their desirable shapes with the passing years, and corrective measures must be taken to restore them to attractive form. Some tend to grow lean and rangy. These must be tightened up. Here we reverse the rule and cut back the offending stems to inward-facing buds, to throw the growth that way. We also cut back more severely than usual to make the branching start as low as possible. Then if the new shoots are again too rangy, we cut them back—but not so far—the following year—to force additional branching. And so on until the shrub has the desired outline.

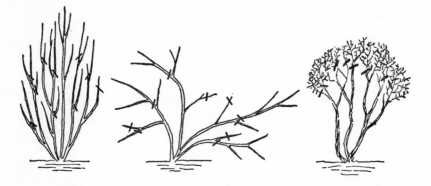

Left, *rose of Sharon* (*too tight*). Center, *flowering quince* (*too loose*). Right, *blueberry* (*top too twiggy*)

If the growth is already too tight, we reverse the process and cut out branches, here and there, to open it up and give it more grace, removing the branches completely or, cutting back to buds that face outward, if necessary to leave a short piece of the branch. In choosing which branches to remove we start by taking out dead stems, then tired, old, twiggy ones that show little new growth. Finally, we remove those that are crowding others, cross over and shade others, or otherwise interfere with branches we want.

On young, fast-growing shrubs and established ones in the warmer areas, it is often advisable to add an intermediate pruning—summer pinching. This nipping off with thumb and fingernail of the last two or three inches of the shoots tends to ripen the wood and cause the setting of buds. If done toward the end of summer it seldom forces new growth. The only plants that should not be so treated are flowering-sized tip bloomers such as lilacs and viburnums.

TO IMPROVE THE BLOOM

As shrubs grow older many tend to become dense at the tips. This can happen to spireas, blueberries used for ornament, honeysuckles, and many others. The cure is to remove the dense, twiggy growths. This allows more light to get in and reduces the competition for nourishment. Again, the amount to cut back is a matter of judgment but remember that the farther you cut such a stem back the greater your risk of throwing the new shoots into stem and leaf growth at the expense of bloom.

Another simple but effective way of improving bloom is to remove all seed pods as soon as they begin to form. Any strength that goes into the formation of seeds necessarily comes from within the plant. This deprives the plant of that much sustenance which could go into growth and buds for another year. Pod removal is especially important on such heavy seed setters as lilacs and kolkwitzia, or beautybush.

PRUNING TO REJUVENATE

After a time all shrubs get old; the stems not only become twiggy but lose their vigor. Growth begins to look unkempt and flowering decreases. This is the time to revive or reawaken such shrubs. As we described above, the bushy old growth must be removed but this time, not just the tips but the whole stems, usually as close to the ground as possible. This permits new, vigorous shoots to take their place. Usually, for appearance's sake we don't do this all at once although it can be done. We normally take about one-third of the oldest and worst stems out the first year, the same number the second, and the rest the third.

Both tender and hardy sorts are included here. Some that are evergreens in warm climates are included here but many, especially the hardier shrubs, will be found in the chapter on evergreens.

*Abelia—***Abelia**
FORM: Arching yet compact.
USES: Borders, foundation plantings, informal hedges, specimens. West Coast and South up to New York.
CARE: Light snipping to maintain form except when hedge. Prune fall, warm areas; spring, cold.

*Abutilon—***Flowering Maple**
FORM: Straggling, thin.
USES: Alone, against walls, in pots in North.
CARE: Cut back to strong wood to keep compact, able to stand alone. Fall or spring, warm areas.

*Acacia—***Mimosa**
FORM: Weakish, sprawling.
USES: Specimens, standards outdoors and cool greenhouse.
CARE: Will stand hard cutting for compactness if shrub, shearing if standard. After bloom.

*Acanthopanax—***Five-leaved Aralia**
FORM: Upright, gracefully arching.
USES: Borders, foundations, specimens, loose hedges.
CARE: Light trimming for guidance while resting.

*Adenocarpus—***Canary Island Lupin**
FORM: Loose, straggling.

USES: Hedges, against walls, specimens.
CARE: Usually nip to shape, prevent seeds. Can stand hard shaping. After blooming in mild climates.

*Aesculus—***Buckeye**
FORM: Compact hemisphere.
USES: Specimens, broad low screens.
CARE: Little except to shape. When dormant.

*Amelanchier—***Shadbush, Serviceberry**
FORM: Open, arching; small trees.
USES: Semiwild masses.
CARE: Minimum. After blooming.

*Arbutus unedo—***Strawberry Tree**
FORM: Neat, compact evergreen.
USES: General plantings, specimens, small trees.
CARE: Minimum for shaping, height control. Spring, when growth starts in warm areas.

*Ardisia—***Ardisia**
FORM: Neat, compact low evergreen.
USES: Specimens, general plantings, pot plants, for berries.
CARE: Minimum for shaping. Under glass, North.

*Aronia—***Chokeberry**
FORM: Spreading, thin.

USES: Natural plantings.
CARE: Head to encourage branching. When berries fall.

Aucuba—**Gold-Dust Tree**
FORM: Compact, well-branched.
USES: In tubs indoors or out, specimens, foundation plantings. Deep South, West Coast.
CARE: Tip-pinch to force out branches, cut hard to renew old plants. Take out dead wood after frost outdoors, late spring.

Azalea—**Azalea**
FORM: Compact to straggling depending upon species.
USES: Specimens; foundation, border, or natural plantings; pots.
CARE: Cut just above joint to thicken sparingly branched sorts, cut to ground stems that have outlived usefulness.

Azara—**Azara**
FORM: Rather open; arching stems.
USES: Excellent for espaliering; specimens in mild climates.
CARE: Stands severe cutting, although shaping usually enough.

Bambusa—**Bamboo**
FORM: Usually in tight clumps.
USES: Screen plantings, hedges, specimens. Mild areas.
CARE: In spring cut to or just below ground, if thinning or rejuvenation needed.

Bauhinia—**Bauhinia**
FORM: *B. galpini*, semiclimbing; *B. variegata*, loose, open.

USES: Specimens, espaliers, standards.
CARE: For training only, spring. After blooming.

Berberis—**Barberry**
FORM: Dense, bushy.
USES: Mostly hedges, some borders.
CARE: Spring, for shaping in border. Shear as necessary any time in hedge.

Bouvardia—**Bouvardia**
FORM: Rapid grower, spreading.
USES: Low trellises, border plantings, specimens.
CARE: Renew wood by thinning, heading. Will bloom all year if pruned severely each year after heavy blooming period. Second pruning if desired in absence of frosts.

Buddleia—**Butterfly Bush**
FORM: Vigorous, open, spreading.
USES: Specimen for blooms, border.
CARE: Cold climates, cut to ground each spring. Warm, cut back hard, thin, remove oldest stems after flowering.

Calliandra—**Trinidad Flame Bush**
FORM: Feather-like, open.
USES: Specimens.
CARE: Pinch tips in spring, summer, to prevent legginess.

Callicarpa—**Beautyberry**
FORM: Rounded, upright, somewhat arching.
USES: In borders for berries on new wood.

CARE: In cold climates cut hard, early spring. If freezes back, cut to ground. Warm areas, cut hard for fruit after berries are gone.

Callistemon—Bottle Brush
FORM: Slender, semiweeping.
USES: Espaliers, specimens, tubs.
CARE: Very little. Pinch tips while young to shape. Does not branch readily from old wood —do not cut to bare stems. Fall.

Calluna—Scottish Heather
FORM: Low, shrubby; leggy if overfed.
USES: Likes poor soil, banks.
CARE: Cut back as necessary, early spring, to shape and for bloom.

Caragana—Siberian Pea Tree
FORM: Open, straggling.
USES: Specimens, hedges.
CARE: Cut out old wood, shorten branches. Cut severely every few years after bloom.

Carissa—Natal Plum
FORM: Irregular.
USES: Hedges, specimens, tubs.
CARE: Start early—branches on ground at first. Head new growth for strong framework; late spring.

Caryopteris—Bluebeard
FORM: Generally shapely.
USES: Specimens, shrub borders.
CARE: Cold climates, cut to ground each spring. Mild areas, cut hard in fall to bush out.

Cassia—Cassia
FORM: Spreading, large.

USES: Specimens.
CARE: Develop framework when young. After blooming cut season's growth back to short spurs.

Catalpa—Umbrella Catalpa
FORM: Small tree.
USES: Specimens for drooping effects.
CARE: Do not cut trunk. Cut back top to short spurs when dormant.

Ceratostigma—Plumbago
FORM: More or less trailing.
USES: Naturalistic uses.
CARE: For early flowers, cut back one-third when dormant. For later bloom, cut to ground.

Chaenomeles—Flowering Quince
FORM: Compact, or loose and straggly.
Uses: Foundation or border planting; specimens.
CARE: Thin out tight, nonflowering growth. Cut back after flowering to make loose ones bushy.

Chamaelaucium—Geraldton Wax Flower
FORM: Open, graceful.
USES: Natural plantings.
CARE: Cut flowers freely. Cut severely after flowering, leaving spurs of new wood.

Choisya—Mexican Orange
FORM: Compact, thick.
USES: Hedges, borders, specimens, pot plants.
CARE: Stands heavy cutting. Cut back hard on shabby ones. Otherwise, thin and trim lightly after blooming.

*Chorizema—***Flowering Oak**
FORM: Trailer.
USES: Over walls, low trellises, ground covers.
CARE: After bloom take out dead wood. Cut back to prevent seeds, force new growth.

*Cistus—***Rockrose**
FORM: Compact or trailing.
USES: Bank and naturalistic plantings, ground covers.
CARE: Very little. Head back to side branches if leggy, but not to bare wood.

*Clerodendron—***Glory Bower**
FORM: Large, compact.
USES: Specimens, general borders.
CARE: Thin dense plants. Remove winter damage early spring.

*Clethra—***Summersweet**
FORM: Thick, many-stemmed clumps.
USES: Naturalistic and border plantings.
CARE: Occasional thinning or training.

*Cornus—***Dogwood**
FORM: Moderately shapely.
USES: General borders, naturalistic plantings.
CARE: *Cornus mas,* slight training or thinning after blooming. Colored stemmed sorts, cut hard and often to ground for vigorous new growth. Spring.

*Corylopsis—***Winter Hazel**
FORM: Much-branched, compact.
USES: General plantings.

CARE: Occasional thinning, training after blooming.

*Cotoneaster—***Cotoneaster, Rockspray**
FORM: Most are fairly vigorous.
USES: Hedges, ground covers, bank plantings, wall plants.
CARE: General training. If leggy, cut back. If twiggy, unvigorous, cut hard for new shoots. Early spring.

*Daphne—***Garland Flower**
FORM: Reasonably compact.
USES: *D. cneorum.* Base plantings, rock gardens. Others, general.
CARE: Training to maintain shape during or after blooming.

*Deutzia—***Deutzia**
FORM: Often dense, twiggy.
USES: Specimens, general plantings.
CARE: Thin when twiggy. Needs occasional hard cutting of oldest stems, often to ground, to force new shoots.

*Duranta—***Sky Flower**
FORM: Somewhat arching, rampant.
USES: Specimens.
CARE: Cut back stems that fruited back to ground or to strong laterals that have not yet fruited. Spring. Do not prune tips.

*Elaeagnus—***Russian Olive, Silverberry**
FORM: Broad, spreading, but neat.
USES: Specimens, hedges.
CARE: Slight training usually, but stands heavy cutting.

*Elsholtzia—***Mintshrub**
FORM: Half-woody.
USES: General plantings.
CARE: Cut back, end of winter, to remove dead portions. Stands cutting to ground if necessary.

*Enkianthus—***Enkianthus**
FORM: Open, leggy.
USES: In plantings with rhododendrons, etc.
CARE: Cut back judiciously after blooming to thicken up.

*Erica—***Heather**
FORM: Usually compact.
USES: Mass plantings; in pots.
CARE: After blooming cut back to unflowered stems. Remove old knuckles. Shear back dwarf forms.

*Escallonia—***Escallonia**
FORM: Compact, twiggy.
USES: Hedges, borders, wall plants, specimens.
CARE: Cut back, thin severely. Remove one-fourth (oldest) stems to ground after flowering. Cut laterals back to short spurs.

*Eugenia—***Australian Brush Cherry**
FORM: Tall, erect, weakish-stemmed.
USES: Hedges, tubs, specimens.
CARE: Top to regulate height. Cut back to lighten branches, prevent breakage of weak crotches. Spring.

*Euonymus—***Burning Bush**
FORM: Shrubby sorts reasonably compact.

USES: General plantings, hedges, specimens.
CARE: Thin occasionally to maintain vigorous branches, shape. Stands heavy cutting for hedges.

*Euphorbia—***Poinsettia**
FORM: Spreading, open.
USES: Specimens, espaliers.
CARE: Cut back year-old wood to short spurs in spring, leaving one or two buds per spur. On older plants, remove knuckles.

*Exochorda—***Pearlbush**
FORM: Somewhat open, spreading.
USES: General plantings, specimens.
CARE: Head back to compact. Thinning seldom necessary. After flowering.

*Fatsia—***Ricepaper Plant**
FORM: Clumps of straight stems with umbrella-like heads.
USES: Specimens, tub plants.
CARE: Remove fruiting bodies. Remove oldest canes to ground. Spring.

*Feijoa—***Feijoa**
FORM: Compact.
USES: Tub plants, specimens.
CARE: Cut for shaping. Remove frozen parts but not until new buds develop well along in late spring.

*Ficus—***Rubber Plant**
FORM: Can get leggy.
USES: Tub plants, specimens.
CARE: Head back as necessary to shape. Any time.

*Fontanesia—***Syrian Privet**
FORM: Slender, willowy, privet-like.
USES: Hedges, general plantings. Drought resistant.
CARE: Head in for compactness or hedging. Early spring.

*Forsythia—***Goldenbells**
FORM: Upright or arching.
USES: Specimens; foundation and border plantings.
CARE: Thin out weak old shoots to ground. Shape. After flowering.

*Fothergilla—***Fothergilla**
FORM: Many-stemmed, bushy.
USES: Early bloom, mostly in naturalistic plantings.
CARE: Thin occasionally by removing weakest, oldest stems to ground after flowering.

*Fuchsia—***Fuchsia**
FORM: Vigorous, semiwoody, half-climbers.
USES: Specimens, hedges, pillars, standards, espaliers, vines.
CARE: Cut back severely to short, sturdy spurs. Thin out. Winter, if frost-free; late spring elsewhere. Pinch tips during growth.

*Grevillea—***Jewelflower**
FORM: Compact, softish.
USES: Border plantings, specimens. *G. robusta* often a pot plant.
CARE: Resent cutting. Cut only to train.

*Hakea—***Hakea**
FORM: Dense, rounded, on sometimes leggy stems.

USES: Hedges, specimens, borders in dry places.
CARE: Young plants, pinch tips to bush out. Do not shear; slow to recover, does not branch well from old wood.

*Hamamelis—***Witch Hazel**
FORM: Straggling shrub or small tree.
USES: Naturalistic plantings, borders.
CARE: Trim to shape and produce flowering branchlets. Spring.

Hebe (Veronica)—**Hebe**
FORM: Compact, well-shaped.
USES: Formal or informal hedge, borders, specimens.
CARE: Can be held to any height. Occasionally remove oldest stems to ground, train new ones. After main bloom.

*Heteromeles—***Toyon**
FORM: Round, compact.
USES: Naturalistic plantings, borders, specimens.
CARE: Stands heavy pruning but shaping usually enough. Spring.

Hibiscus (tender)—**Chinese Hibiscus**
FORM: Open.
USES: Specimens, general planting.
CARE: Cut back hard, if necessary, to strong laterals for new flower wood.

Hibiscus (hardy)—**Rose of Sharon**
FORM: Narrow, dense, upright.
USES: Specimens, informal hedges, borders.
CARE: Blooms on new wood. Needs

thinning to open up. The harder cut back, the better the flowers. Spring.

Holodiscus—Rock Spirea
FORM: Gracefully arching branches.
USES: General plantings.
CARE: In cold climates remove winter damage. Shape after bloom.

Hydrangea (tender)—Hydrangea
FORM: Round, dense.
USES: Specimens, low borders, in pots for indoors.
CARE: Cut back to strong, unflowered laterals. Leave unflowered shoots unless too thick. After bloom. Cut to ground when old.

Hydrangea (hardy)—Hydrangea
FORM: P.G., large, coʻrse; Hills-of-Snow, more shapely.
USES: Standards, borders; Specimens.
CARE: Shape, thin. Stand heavy cutting—to two to four bud spurs on standards or to ground for renewal. Spring.

Hypericum—St.-John's-Wort
FORM: Straggly and spreading to compact and twiggy.
USES: Borders, low informal hedges, foundation plantings.
CARE: Thin and shape. Remove old and weak shoots. Groundcover sorts can be cut to ground when old. Spring, when growth starts.

Kerria—Japanese Kerria
FORM: Slender-branched, spreading.
USES: Foundation plantings, borders, specimens.
CARE: Cut back new and remove oldest canes to ground. Thin, at ground level, if necessary. After flowering.

Kolkwitzia—Beautybush
FORM: Tall, upright.
USES: Borders, specimens.
CARE: Prune out oldest canes occasionally, top young ones if too tall. After blooming.

Lagerstroemia—Crape Myrtle
FORM: Somewhat open.
USES: Specimens; foundation and border plantings.
CARE: Blooms profusely on new wood. Head back in early spring to compact growth. Remove damaged wood. Where freezes back severely cut to ground.

Leptospermum—Australian Tea
FORM: Sprawling.
USES: Windbreaker, hedges, borders, specimens.
CARE: Train while young, cutting heavily to force growth upward. Does not throw shoots readily from old wood. Shape any time. Cut hard when resting.

Ligustrum—Privet
FORM: Strong, upright or spreading.
USES: Hedges primarily, sometimes borders or specimens.
CARE: Cut back any time for hedge,

when dormant if trained naturally. Stands any amount of cutting. Good for topiary work.

Lonicera—**Honeysuckle**
FORM: Strong but neat, bushy.
USES: Foundation and border plantings, hedges, screens, specimens.
CARE: Thin out, remove oldest canes to ground in early spring every five to six years.

Magnolia—**Magnolia**
FORM: Reasonably shapely.
USES: Specimens, shrub borders.
CARE: Prune as little as possible to shape. Does not need much and does not heal easily. After flowers.

Melaleuca—**Bottlebrush**
FORM: Open, straggly.
USES: Specimens mostly: shrub borders.
CARE: Head when young to bush out but not too far. Does not sprout easily from older stems. Spring.

Myrsine—**African Boxwood**
FORM: Compact, leafy.
USES: Formal or informal hedges; specimens.
CARE: Little cutting necessary, but stands severe cutting if desired, even to ground. Preferably when resting.

Myrica—**Bayberry**
FORM: Bushy, compact.
USES: Borders, naturalistic plantings, especially in sand.
CARE: Little necessary but a little thinning helps prevent dead wood. After berries are cut or in spring.

Nerium—**Oleander**
FORM: Tall, slender, arching.
USES: Specimens, standards, tubbed, informal hedges.
CARE: Top and root prune to hold down, if too tall. Remove old wood that has flowered. Sucker tree type. Spring.

Pernettya—**Broadleaf Pernettya**
FORM: Low (18″). Compact in sun, straggly in shade.
USES: Fruiting ground cover.
CARE: Head back to shape if straggly. Early spring.

Philadelphus—**Mock Orange**
FORM: Stout, arching.
USES: Specimens, borders, screens.
CARE: Occasional trim for shaping, except when necessary to renew. Then cut oldest stems to ground. After flowering.

Photinia—**Photinia**
FORM: Tall, leggy, round-headed.
USES: Specimens, borders, for berries.
CARE: Cut back both evergreen and nonevergreen sorts occasionally to compact. After flowering. Better a few stems at a time.

Physocarpus—**Ninebark**
FORM: Large, spreading.
USES: Foundation and border plantings.
CARE: Renew from base by cutting a few oldest stems to ground each year after flowering.

*Pimelea—***Rice Flower**
FORM: Somewhat conelike, compact.
USES: Specimens.
CARE: Does not like severe pruning. Trim after flowering.

*Pittosporum—***Pittosporum**
FORM: Well-shaped, compact, some weeping at tips.
USES: Borders, formal or informal hedges, windbreaks, tub plants. Drought resistant.
CARE: Stands severe pruning. Can be kept any height. Head back any time in warm regions. Spring in colder.

*Polygala—***Milkwort**
FORM: Neat, compact domes.
USES: Borders, specimens.
CARE: Stands severe pruning. Usually trimmed lightly in late summer, after heaviest flowering.

*Prunus—***Flowering Almonds, Plums**
FORM: Reasonably compact.
USES: Specimens, borders, foundation plantings.
CARE: Trim after bloom to maintain shape. Cut oldest stems out occasionally to rejuvenate.

*Punica—***Pomegranate**
FORM: Compact shrubs or small trees.
USES: Hedges, specimens, pot plants indoors.
CARE: Remove old, twiggy, and weak branches. Head back new growth each winter to encourage flowering.

*Pyracantha—***Firethorn**
FORM: Often sprawling.
USES: Specimens, border and foundation plantings; hedges, often espaliered.
CARE: Stands heavy cutting if desired. Otherwise, tip-pinch any time. When taking berries cut back to unflowered laterals. For most berries cut all wood that fruited. After berries drop.

*Raphiolepis—***Yeddo Hawthorn**
FORM: Well-compacted.
USES: Tub plants, specimens, espaliers, ground covers.
CARE: Remove straggling branches and dead, or interfering ones. Stands hard pruning but rarely necessary.

*Rhodotypos—***Jetbead**
FORM: May get straggly.
USES: Foundation plantings, borders.
CARE: Prune back severely when necessary to keep compact. Take out oldest canes every few years to rejuvenate. After berries gone.

*Rhus—***Smoketree**
FORM: Large, rounded.
USES: Specimens, large borders.
CARE: Slight shaping in early spring.

*Ribes—***Flowering Currant**
FORM: Compact, bushy.
USES: Natural plantings, borders.
CARE: Renew by removing old and weak shoots to ground in early fall but do not head back or flowers will be cut off. To shape golden currant, cut after flowers.

*Robinia—***Locust**
FORM: Irregular. Suckers into clumps.
USES: Specimens, borders.
CARE: Needs heading back after flowering to compact. Thin occasionally. Remove excess suckers.

*Rosa—***Shrub Roses**
FORM: Generally bushy clumps.
USES: Hedges, borders, backgrounds for flowers.
CARE: Thin and rejuvenate as needed.

*Rosmarinus—***Rosemary**
FORM: Low, bushy.
USES: Low hedges, tub plants.
CARE: Trim lightly in summer to shape and remove old flowers.

*Shepherdia—***Buffalo Berry**
FORM: Large, not especially dense.
USES: General plantings, especially in North Central States.
CARE: Occasional guidance after flowering.

*Sorbaria—***False Spirea**
FORM: Suckers into large clumps.
USES: Borders, informal plantings.
CARE: Occasional thinning to ground, and guidance for shape. Early spring.

*Spiraea—***Spirea**
FORM: Graceful arching fountains to compact shrubs.
USES: Foundation plantings, borders, specimens, hedges.
CARE: Cut to shape if needed. Thin out old and weak canes to ground. There are so many spi-

raeas that the safest rule is to prune them all after flowering.

*Stephanandra—***Stephanandra**
FORM: Graceful, spreading.
USES: Low borders, in front of larger shrubs, foundation plantings.
CARE: Thin out wood that has flowered, cutting to strong laterals or ground. Spring. Tips may freeze in cold climates.

*Symphoricarpos—***Snowberry, Coral-Berry**
FORM: Loose, spreading, open.
USES: Foundation plantings, borders, informal plantings.
CARE: Thin out old and overcrowded canes to ground. Shape as needed in early spring.

*Syringa—***Lilac**
FORM: Strong, shapely, round-topped, single- or several-stemmed.
USES: Borders, screens, specimens.
CARE: Remove seedheads, thin or shape as necessary after flowering. Rejuvenate old plants by removing one-third of all canes or branches each year for three years. If a grafted plant, remove all suckers.

*Tamarix—***Tamarisk**
FORM: Rather arching or sprawling.
USES: Ground covers, naturalistic and border plantings, specimens.
CARE: Prune spring-flowering kinds after blooming; summer-flowering, head back hard while dor-

mant. Cut all to ground when necessary to rejuvenate.

Teucrium—**Teucrium**
FORM: Low, sprawling.
USES: Low hedges and edgings, specimens.
CARE: Takes severe cutting. Head back to shape. To renew, cut to ground. Fall.

Tibouchina—**Lasiandra**
FORM: Erect, rangy.
USES: Wall plants, specimens, greenhouse plants.
CARE: Cut out weak stems, head back to strong buds. Late spring. If freezes, wait until new growth starts before cutting out dead wood.

Vaccinium—**Blueberry**
FORM: Bushy, twiggy.
USES: Borders, screens, naturalistic plantings.
CARE: Thin out old, twiggy stems to ground if necessary. Shape as desired when dormant.

Viburnum—**Viburnum**
FORM: A large and variable group.

USES: All purposes.
CARE: Stand any cutting necessary to maintain shape or bush out. Thin top or to ground as desired, if too thick. After blooming. Often grafted; remove suckers.

Vitex—**Chaste Tree**
FORM: Large, bushy.
USES: Specimens, borders.
CARE: Kills back in severe winters. Remove damage as soon as sure, to ground if necessary. Severe cutting back improves blooming.

Weigela—**Weigela**
FORM: Arching, rounded.
USES: Borders and foundation plantings, specimens.
CARE: Remove older stems. Cut back flowered wood to strong unflowered laterals. Thin. Pinch tips if straggling. After blooming.

Zanthorhiza—**Yellowroot**
FORM: Low (1–2'), spreading by suckers.
USES: Ground cover under trees.
CARE: No pruning except to check spreading.

VI. How to Handle Evergreens

In some ways the pruning of evergreens differs from that of deciduous or leaf-dropping plants. Evergreens do drop their leaves, but not all at once. Therefore we must aim at all times to keep as much of the foliage undamaged as possible. Also, many evergreens, especially those of larger size, do not readily throw out new branches after cutting.

WHY PRUNE?

As a group, evergreens need less pruning than broad-leaved plants—especially the needle-leaved evergreens. Often they need little more than shaping, whether they be trees or hedges. In the case of the broad-leaved evergreens—rhododendrons, hollies, camellias, and so on—we must keep in mind both the form of the plant and the aim of increasing the number of flowers and berries. In the shrubby forms, too, we sometimes find it necessary to reduce legginess. In our discussion here, we shall omit the strictly fruit types, as the citrus group, and take them up later in Chapter XI.

AND WHEN?

Since some evergreens, the spruces and pines especially, do not branch out readily after cutting, timing is of particular importance. If any serious cutting must be done, it should be completed before the growth has finished for the year. Still better is to do it just before the new growth starts or is still in its early stages. Then the new adventitious buds have a chance to form and lead shoots will not remain empty stubs that will die back through lack of growing points.

Arborvitae, hemlock, false cypress, yew, juniper, and similar species can be trimmed lightly almost any time. Heavier pruning, however, is better confined to shortly before or just as growth commences in spring, not because it is necessary for the formation of buds but so that the trees may outgrow their "haircut" appearance as soon as possible. The same is true of pines and spruces when given only a light touching up.

So far in our discussion of when to prune, we have mentioned only the season, not how to handle young or old specimens. This is because, unlike most plants, evergreens rarely need any cutting when planted. Young ones come from the nursery in cans or balled and burlapped instead of bare-root; therefore they suffer little root loss to be balanced by pruning. Also, if they needed any guiding in their early stages they received it from the nurseryman. They come to you, the gardener, already in proper form.

Flowering and berry-bearing evergreens are handled somewhat differently. Those such as rhododendrons, pieris, laurels, and others that go into the dormant period with their fat flower buds already formed, are cut immediately after blooming. Those that produce their flower buds later on new wood, such as the usual hollies, may be cut any time during the dormant period or, if berry-bearing, as soon as the fruits are ripe. Then they may be picked for indoor use, thus accomplishing some trimming back at the same time.

SHEARING VERSUS PRUNING

Many people confuse these operations. Shearing is giving the plant a general haircut as you would a hedge, with a large pair of scissor-like shears. These are held at the proper angle and distance and everything that sticks out beyond that is cut off.

Pruning, on the other hand, involves selection and judgment. Since hemlocks, arborvitae, plume cypresses, yews, and upright junipers produce a large number of small shoots at the tips of the branches, pruning tip by tip is tedious and these are often sheared. However, this produces a stiff, formal look. A much better way is to take a light pruning shear or knife and singly or a few at a time cut those tips that project beyond the desired outline. The technique is slower than shearing but it produces a softer, more natural look instead of the "billiard balls," "inverted ice cream cones," or "lollipops" one so often sees.

Left, *evergreens sheared.* Right, *pruned*

Pines, spruces, firs, and other "whorl"-type growers do not lend themselves to shearing. All such plants should be pruned by judicious cut-by-cut methods—preferably even when they are reduced to formal hedges. Low, spreading yews and junipers, such as Pfitzer's, are also best trained by individual cuts.

OVERGROWN SPECIMENS

Occasionally one is advised not to cut more than the annual growth on either kind of evergreen. At least a small portion of the current wood, one is told, should be left. This is sheer (and shear) nonsense! I have cut freely a great many times on fine-branched evergreens (arborvitae, plume cypresses, etc.) with never any harm resulting.

There are many cases where severe cutting must be done, such as when the plants have been left untended for so long that the foundation planting completely obscures one's house windows. I myself have cut—all but the yews—back from twelve to thirteen feet to eight or nine. The only thing that must then be done is to work down carefully over the whole plant to restore it to its pyramidal form.

There are two further details in restoring old evergreen trees of this type. Remember not to cut the bottom branches off the trunk!

They cannot be grown back on. The method of growing the plant a new point will be described below.

THE EXCEPTIONS

The only other thing to keep in mind about shearing, pruning, and cutting back, as described above, is not to do it to firs, spruces, and especially pines. These produce branches in whorls or clusters at the same level around the trunk, or around the branches. To head these back gently and produce bushing out, as you might want in a formal white pine hedge, take out the central bud, or "candle," after it has begun to grow. This can be done year after year, if desired, without harm.

Left, *lateral shoot showing where to cut to thicken growth* (*pine*). Right, *how to train new leader* (*fir*)

If such cutting is required on nonhedge specimens the year's new leaders can be cut back, but this must be done before the lengthening has ceased for the year. This usually takes place by midsummer. Then, new buds have time to form and the stubs do not die.

Still more severe cutting back may be practiced by removing the entire central leaders on each branch. This causes their mates to bush out. Only the tree's central leader needs different care. It is cut to a stub, one of its neighbors in the nearest whorl must be tied upright to it until it stands upright itself in its place, after which the stub is removed entirely. This slows down vertical growth somewhat and lets the tree fill out more in the meantime. The same technique is also practiced when the tree is without a leader because of insect injury or accident. If no stub is present, tie the new leader to a splint tied to the trunk. In fact, in spite of much advice to the contrary, as much as three years' growth can often be cut off in this way. If done carefully, the cutting and training is a big boon to older, overgrown, or misshapen plants.

BROAD-LEAVED EVERGREENS

In general, these, too, usually do not need as much pruning as deciduous plants, but a little occasional guidance or correction is necessary. On camellias, hollies, and most others the same principles hold except that the plants do not put out buds as readily from really old stems. Hence, they are rarely cut back as severely as deciduous plants.

Enough of what is not done. Now for what is done.

(1) Many fine-stemmed kinds, of which the Japanese hollies (*Ilex crenata*) are a good example, stand considerable cutting. This may be in the form of shearing like a hedge or judicious overall pruning, both for the purpose of maintaining the desired form.

The larger-leaved, more treelike evergreens, represented by the English and American hollies, can be cut back farther than is generally expected, to cause new branching. Still, for practical purposes, it is safer for the amateur not to cut back any wood over three and especially over four years old.

(2) Coarser growers such as rhododendrons and mountain laurel

Left, *how to rejuvenate leggy or damaged rhododendrons.* Right, *seed head of rhododendron*

require very little cutting to keep them in line. Still, occasionally a branch reaches too far out and must be headed back. In such a case it is better not to cut back beyond three-year-old wood, always cutting back to just above some leaves or dormant buds.

(3) Sometimes these same shrubs get too leggy and need to be shortened. This can be done by the method of the preceding paragraph, except that the cutting back is more general.

(4) In extreme cases where shortening is not sufficiently effective, plants can be cut back to the ground and entirely new heads allowed to grow up. But before you try these drastic measures make sure your plants can survive such ruthless beheading. It works very well on rhododendrons, azaleas, mountain laurel, pieris, leucothoe, and similar plants. In fact, it is the usual practice of nurserymen who sell stock gathered in our southern mountains. The plants are dug, the tops cut to the ground, the plants put out in rows, and new tops grown on them before they are sold.

(5) When rhododendrons and similar plants get too old and need rejuvenation, cutting back as described in paragraph 4 is practical.

(6) Lastly, to avoid the strength of the plant being wasted in the production of seeds instead of growth or flowers for next year, all developing seed heads are removed. This should be done as early as possible, by taking the head between thumb and one finger and bending it over sharply until it snaps off.

ROAD MAP TO PRUNING EVERGREENS—BY KINDS

Both hardy and tender sorts are included here. However, those bearing edible fruits are listed under fruit trees and a great many tender shrubby sorts have already been treated under shrubs, since some that are evergreen in mild climates become deciduous in colder ones.

Abies—Fir
FORM: Tall, gracefully pyramidal. Needle-leaved.
USES: Specimens in cooler regions, hedges.
CARE: Whorl-type growth. Prune with care, soon after growth starts.

Andromeda—Bog Rosemary
FORM: Small, low, spreading.
USES: Fillers between rhodos, azaleas, etc. Cooler regions.

CARE: Thin or shape if necessary. After flowering.

Arbutus menziesi—Madrone
FORM: Compact, round-headed, treelike.
USES: Specimens. Warm climates.
CARE: Little needed. Head back if necessary, but not too hard. Spring, as growth commences.

Arctostaphylos—Bearberry, Kinnick-kinnick
FORM: Low, spreading (6–8″).
USES: Ground cover in sandy, rocky, well-drained places.
CARE: Very little except for guidance. Rarely, if ever, too tall.

Araucaria—Monkey Puzzle
FORM: Tall, pyramidal tree with open, whirly growth. Needled.
USES: Specimens, curiosities. Warm climates. Pots indoors.
CARE: As little as possible. Do not cut leader without replacing.

Azalea—Azalea
FORM: Shrubs, generally less leggy, more bushy than leaf-dropping relatives.
USES: Specimens, foundations, borders, naturalistic plantings, in pots.
CARE: Head rangy branches, especially those that would hide flowers, by cutting back to joint. Thin out too-twiggy branches or, if bad, cut to ground. After flowering. Remove seed pods.

Buxus—Boxwood
FORM: Dense, bushy shrubs; fine-twigged, fine-leaved.

USES: Specimens, hedges, foundation plantings.
CARE: Remove dead wood. Shear as growth commences. Branches easily from old wood, can be cut back hard.

Camellia—Camellia
FORM: Shapely shrubs; broad leaves.
USES: Specimens, cut flowers, hedges, espaliers, general plantings. Pots indoors.
CARE: Thin out old, twiggy growth. Head back gently, if needed. Remove old flowers. Can be cut severely after flowering.

Carpenteria—Carpenteria
FORM: Shrub (6–10′).
USES: Border and foundation plantings in dry, sandy places. Suited to West Coast and East, north to Philadelphia.
CARE: Guide growth, remove frost injury and suckers in spring.

Cedrus—True Cedars
FORM: Tall, needle-leaved pyramids with horizontal branches.
USES: Specimens, screens. (In northern zones, move in June.)
CARE: Trim lightly for guidance. Do not cut leader without replacing.

Cephalotaxus—Plum Yew
FORM: Yewlike, spreading, to 30 feet high. Branches may droop.
USES: Screens, borders, specimens, hedges.
CARE: Trim, if necessary, to shape. Spring.

*Chamaecyparis—***Retinospora, Plume Cypress**
FORM: Mostly narrow pyramids. Fine-needled.
USES: Boundary, foundation plantings; specimens, hedges.
CARE: Stands shearing if needed to hold down or shape.

*Citrus trifoliata—***Hardy Orange**
FORM: Small, spreading, broad-leaved tree.
USES: General plantings, hedges. Hardy to zero or lower.
CARE: May be cut severely.

*Cryptomeria—***Cryptomeria**
FORM: Tall, narrowly pyramidal. Sequoia-like needles.
USES: Specimens, accents, boundary plantings.
CARE: Stands trimming for guidance.

*Cunninghamia—***China Fir**
FORM: Broad pyramid, spreading branches, drooping at ends. Needled.
USES: Specimens.
CARE: Stands guidance. Sprouts even from stumps.

*Dombeya—***Pinkball**
FORM: Treelike, broad-leaved shrub.
USES: General plantings, borders.
CARE: Stands reasonable guidance. Remove old flowers. Spring.

*Euonymus—***Euonymus**
FORM: Shrubs and creepers, broad-leaved.

USES: Ground cover, wall plants, specimens, hedges.
CARE: Head too-long shoots, remove old wood, shape or shear. Any time where mild, spring in cold climates.

*Gardenia—***Gardenia**
FORM: Rounded, broad-leaved shrub.
USES: Specimens, general plantings, hedges. Tub and greenhouse.
CARE: Remove weak wood. Thin for better flowers and shape as needed.

*Ilex—***Holly**
FORM: Large-leaved, pyramidal trees and small-leaved, rounded shrubs.
USES: Specimens, border and foundation plantings, hedges.
CARE: Stand reasonable cutting back. Spring, for Christmas berries on some.

*Juniperus—***Juniper, Red Cedar**
FORM: Tall and narrow or low and spreading. Needled.
USES: Accents, foundations, screens, front plantings, hedges.
CARE: Stand considerable shaping or shearing, preferably before growth begins.

*Kalmia—***Mountain Laurel**
FORM: Rounded shrub. Broad-leaved.
USES: Foundations, general and naturalistic plantings.
CARE: May be thinned or thickened after flowering. Cut to ground if straggly. Remove seeds.

*Larix—***Larch**
FORM: Tall pyramidal trees. Needles drop in fall.
USES: Specimens, boundary plantings, summer shade.
CARE: Guide growth if needed. Any time. Restore leader.

*Laurus—***True Laurel**
FORM: Roundheaded, bushy. Broad-leaved.
USES: Tubs, specimens, standards, hedges.
CARE: Stands shearing to any form. Spring. Trim in summer.

*Leucothoe—***Drooping Leucothoe**
FORM: Spreading shrubs (2–5′).
USES: Foundation plantings, with rhodos, under trees.
CARE: May get straggly. Thin or guide as needed after blooming. Cut to ground to rejuvenate.

*Libocedrus—***Incense Cedar**
FORM: Columnar trees, spreading with age. Small-needled.
USES: Specimens, borders.
CARE: Stands shaping, shearing. Spring.

*Ligustrum—***Privet**
FORM: Spreading, broad-leaved shrubs.
USES: Hedges, specimens, general plantings.
CARE: Stands hard shearing any time. Spring for heavy cutting.

*Magnolia—***Magnolia**
FORM: Spreading, large-leaved trees.
USES: Specimens, shade.

CARE: Stand a little guidance. After blooming. Do not heal quickly.

*Mahonia—***Oregon Grape, Holly Grape**
FORM: Mostly broad-spreading shrubs.
USES: Underplantings, foundations, informal hedges.
CARE: Remove winter-burn, old stems. Cut to ground if leggy.

*Michelia—***Banana Shrub**
FORM: Bushy shrubs. Broad-leaved.
USES: Specimens, general plantings.
CARE: Shape if needed. After bloom.

*Myrtus—***True Myrtle**
FORM: Compact broad-leaved shrubs.
USES: Specimens, hedges, borders.
CARE: Leave unpruned or clip formally in spring.

*Nandina—***Heavenly Bamboo**
FORM: Clump of reedlike growth, unbranched.
USES: Tubs, specimens, borders, informal hedges.
CARE: Remove oldest canes. Encourage suckers. Spring.

*Osmanthus—***Sweet Olive**
FORM: Compact shrub. Holly-like leaves but opposite.
USES: Specimens, hedges, pots indoors.
CARE: Little necessary but may be cut hard.

*Picea—***Spruce**
FORM: Tall, pyramidal, needled, branches in whorls.
USES: Specimens, screens, wind-

breaks, boundary plantings, hedges.

CARE: Always provide for one leader unless in hedge. Remove center buds or growth in spring to thicken up branches. Buds easier than pines.

Pieris—Andromea

FORM: Graceful broad-leaved shrubs. Native, upright; Japanese, drooping.

USES: Foreground shrubs with rhodos, foundation plantings, general.

CARE: Seldom necessary but can be cut hard, even to ground, if needed.

Pinus—Pine

FORM: Tall trees, pyramidal when young. Spreading later. Branches in whorls. Long-needled.

USES: Specimens, shade, hedges, windbreaks.

CARE: Always retain leader except in hedges. If necessary to shorten, make new one. Cut it only when growth is starting. Remove branch leaders to thicken.

Podocarpus—Podocarpus

FORM: Usually tall, narrow tree. Long-needled.

USES: Specimens, accents, hedges, pot plant indoors.

CARE: Stands reasonable cutting, best before growth.

Prunus laurocerasus—Cherry Laurel

FORM: Compact bushy shrub. Broad-leaved.

USES: Specimens, informal hedges, tub plants.

CARE: Stands fairly heavy cutting, if needed. Any time.

Pseudolarix—False Larch

FORM: Tall tree. Like larch, drops needles in fall.

USES: Specimens, boundary plantings.

CARE: Little needed. Guide when necessary.

Pseudotsuga—Douglas Fir

FORM: Tall, with down-sweeping branches. Needled.

USES: Specimens, general use.

CARE: Guide, if necessary, especially to form leader when young.

Rhododendron—Rhododendron

FORM: Large, shapely shrubs. Broad-leaved, large or small.

USES: Foundations, screens, general plantings.

CARE: Remove seeds. If leggy cut back to leaf whorl or buds. If generally poor shape, cut to ground.

Sarcococca—Sarcococca

FORM: Neat, compact, broad-leaved shrub.

USES: Specimens, low hedges, in front of rhodos.

CARE: Little needed. Stands shaping, cutting to ground.

Sciadopitys—Umbrella Pine

FORM: Narrow, long-needled tree.

USES: Specimens, accents.

CARE: Little necessary. Can be guided. Spring best.

*Sequoia—***Redwood**
FORM: Giant pyramids, needled. Branches horizontal on young.
USES: Specimens, screens, general use when young.
CARE: Shape if needed.

*Sequoiadendron—***Dawn Redwood**
FORM: Newly rediscovered. Loose pyramid so far. Drops needles.
USES: Specimens, special interest.
CARE: Stands guidance but keep leader.

*Skimmia—***Skimmia**
FORM: Rounded, bushy shrub. Broad-leaved.
USES: Specimens, foundations, evergreen plantings, hedges.
CARE: Rarely needed but guidance possible.

*Taxodium—***Bald Cypress**
FORM: Large. Pyramidal when young, rounded in age. Drops needles.
USES: Large specimens. Swamp not necessary.
CARE: Little needed. Stands guidance. Sprouts from stump.

*Taxus—***Yew**
FORM: Compact, tall or low. Shrubby. Needled.
USES: Hedges, screens, foundation plantings.
CARE: Stands hard cutting, any shape. Best before growth in spring. Light snipping any time.

*Thuja—***Arborvitae**
FORM: Narrow pyramids. Moderate size for evergreen tree. Scaly needles.
USES: Specimens, accents, hedges, screens, foundation plantings.
CARE: Stands hard shearing or even drastic cutting back to reshape if necessary. Before growth in spring.

*Torreya—***Torreya**
FORM: Tall, spreading, somewhat yewlike. Needled. Less treelike in colder climates.
USES: Specimens, general plantings.
CARE: Stands cutting back if needed. Sprouts even from stumps.

*Tsuga—***Hemlock**
FORM: Tall pyramid with graceful sweeping branches. Small needles.
USES: Specimens, screens, borders, hedges.
CARE: Little needed as tree. Can take severe cutting and heading for formal hedge. Before growth best but not necessary.

*Ulex—***Gorse**
FORM: Spiny, branchy shrub (2–4'). Scalelike leaves.
USES: General use, especially at seaside. For evergreen branches.
CARE: May be trimmed for guidance, cut for renewal after flowering.

VII. Hedges

Trimming hedges is perhaps our most widely practiced form of pruning. Certainly, it is the most commonly practiced method of pruning for shape. Basically, we have two forms of hedges: the informal, in which the plants are set out in rows and allowed to grow in more or less their natural forms, with just a little trimming of branches that get too far out of line; and the formal, in which the plants are trained to grow in some architectural form.

When it comes to materials, an unbelievable array presents itself. One of the most interesting hedges I have ever seen is in Stamford, Conn., on the former property of the Bartlett Tree Expert Company. When planting time came the men went off through the woods and gathered seedlings of all the deciduous trees available, mixed them up, and planted them. Under expert care it has become a most unique and effective hedge. While I would hardly recommend this sort of mixture as a general practice, it does show what can be done.

AT PLANTING TIME

When the plants arrive from the nursery they are usually bare-root, except for evergreens, which are more likely to be balled or in cans. The first thing is to freshen the bare-rooted ones by soaking the roots at least overnight in water. Then dig your trench—a continuous trench produces far better results than individual holes and is quicker to dig. It is not within our province here to tell you how to plant the hedge, but obviously it must be planted properly, given good soil, and handled as you would handle any valued shrubs. However, we can take time to note that two rows with the plants staggered usually makes a tighter hedge than a single line.

Before you plant, or immediately after, cut deciduous plants back to within six or eight inches of the ground. This gives the

Left, *newly-planted hedge* (*single line*) *showing how far to cut back*. Right, *planted in double line* (*better*)

roots a chance to get going and also produces bushier tops from the ground up. Evergreens are usually given a preliminary shaping but are not cut back severely, except a few such as hemlock seedlings.

AFTERCARE

It is with formal hedges that most people make the mistake of letting the stems grow up to the desired height or even higher before beginning to shape the hedge. To have a good hedge, well branched to the ground, you must let it grow up slowly, cutting it back by at least six inches every time it grows a foot, and the sides proportionately.

Start early giving your hedge its eventual shape. Do not let the top get wider than the bottom. This shades the lower branches and they never achieve their full vigor. Either keep the sides vertical or make the top narrower than the bottom—this also helps it handle the snow load in cold climates. It matters not whether you have the top flat or rounded. The flat one is easier to cut but less interesting visually. In any case, use a pair of stakes and a heavy line as a guide. Very few amateurs can cut a hedge evenly enough strictly by eye. Once the hedge is established, care consists merely of "haircutting" it back to shape, of trimming it back nearly but not quite to the old wood each time—unless the ends get too twiggy. Then cut back far enough to remove the excess twigginess and start over.

Typical hedge shapes. Extreme left, *undesirable*. Extreme right, *informal*

If the job is small enough you can do it with a pair of conventional hedge shears. If your hedge is a large one you will be happier with an electric hedge trimmer.

EVERGREENS

These are handled differently, because with very few exceptions, such as the boxwoods and small-leaved hollies, they cannot be cut back so severely. The broad-leaved types, camellias and large-leaved hollies, should be trimmed back just enough to keep wayward branches in line and achieve the desired general outline—we discussed this in Chapter VI—always cutting back to a whorl of buds or to small branches on active wood.

Needle-leaved evergreens are treated differently than the broad-leaved. As we mentioned in Chapter VI, fine-twigged sorts such as arborvitae, cedars, yews, hemlocks, plume cypresses, and so on, can either be sheared or pruned fairly heavily. The whorl-branched types especially, and some of the other large-twigged ones—pines, spruces, and firs—need special care. The best way to bush them out is to remove the lead bud or shoot on the tip of every branch each year, by snipping or pinching it out. In either case, these needle-bearing evergreens can be shaped into just as formal effects as deciduous plants if handled with care, and they are far more effective in the landscape for they are on the job all year round.

Some rapid growers like the privets need several cuttings a year —whenever the growth gets too long and they begin to look ragged. The rest of the deciduous sorts will probably get by with perhaps two trimmings a year, before or when new growth is at its height and the plants get out of hand, and again later in the season if they need some shaping. Informal hedges are generally pruned like ordinary shrubs, usually before growth starts in the spring. If they are flowering hedges, trimming is usually postponed until the flowering is over.

The broad-leaved evergreens with small leaves are usually cut back before growth starts in spring and given a light touchup later, if needed. The same is true of the fine-twigged needle-bearers, while the larger, coarser types are best handled just after growth has started in spring (see Chapter VI).

If you find yourself the owner of an old, neglected hedge, you have two choices—assuming it is of the deciduous type—depending upon how far gone it is. If it is not too badly overgrown, you might try cutting it back six inches more than you want the finished hedge on both top and sides and then letting it regrow a new twiggy outside layer in a few easy stages.

On the other hand, if it is badly overgrown, cut it back completely to within six to twelve inches of the ground, using a saw if necessary, and start training it all over. I once brought a twelve- to fourteen-foot privet jungle down to a very presentable sixteen-inch formal edging in a couple of years.

Overgrown hedges of the fine-needled evergreens can often be brought down radically but pines, spruces, and the like are difficult

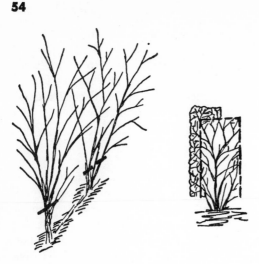

Rejuvenating an old hedge. Left, cut back to 6 inches. Right, old twiggy growth removed

to rejuvenate. In most cases, if they are far gone, it is necessary to pull them out and start all over again with new plants.

PLANTS THAT MAY BE USED FOR HEDGES

Detailed notes on the care of these plants will be found in Chapters V and VI. The following are not *all* the plants that can be grown as hedges; they are simply the most usual ones.

Listed under Shrubs

Abelia	Escallonia	Myrsine
Acacia	Eugenia	Nerium
Acanthopanax	Euonymus	Pittosporum
Adenocarpus	Fontanesia	Punica
Baccharis	Fuchsia	Pyracantha
Berberis	Hakea	Rhamnus
Caragana	Hebe	Rosa
Carissa	Hibiscus	Rosmarinus
Choisya	Hypericum	Spiraea
Cotoneaster	Leptospermum	Teucrium
Elaeagnus	Ligustrum	Viburnum
	Lonicera	

Listed under Evergreens

Abies	*Ilex*	*Pinus*
Buxus	*Juniperus*	*Podocarpus*
Camellia	*Laurus*	*Prunus laurocerasus*
Cephalotaxus	*Ligustrum*	*Sarcococca*
Chamaecyparis	*Mahonia*	*Skimmia*
Citrus trifoliata	*Myrtus*	*Taxus*
Euonymus	*Nandina*	*Thuja*
Gardenia	*Osmanthus*	*Tsuga*
	Picea	

VIII. Roses

In spite of some popular beliefs to the contrary, there is no great mystery about pruning roses. Anyone can do it just as well as he can prune a young apple tree or a flowering quince. Just remember that a rosebush is, after all, a shrub. In mild climates the wood of even the more tender sorts lives through the winter and throws out new growth the following season.

WHEN TO PRUNE

Outside of the usual cutting that accompanies the planting of roses, the time to prune is governed by the climate. In the more southerly states and mild areas along the West Coast where the question of hardiness does not enter, roses are pruned in winter. In many places this means about mid-January or February—in any case when the buds are swelling but just before the plants start into actual growth again. Pruning too early may also cause the stems to die back.

Where cold weather and freezing back must be contended with, pruning is delayed. In the fall each top may be tied into a bundle and shortened to prevent whipping in the wind. In spring, as soon as all danger of freezing back is past, and the mounds of soil used for winter protection are removed, the plants are pruned back at least to live wood.

Modern, large-flowered climbers should get a going over after the flood of spring bloom is past. The old rambler-type climbers are usually cut back after blooming is over. Hardy shrub roses are cut any time during the dormant season or after blooming.

WHEN PLANTING

When you buy roses, they come either dormant and bare-root (this includes the packaged sorts that do not have any real soil around them) or growing in pots or cans, just as most other woody plants. The latter group are merely removed from the containers and set into their permanent locations. They are almost certain to have been pruned properly prior to planting.

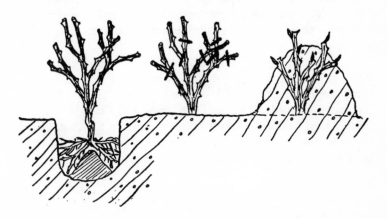

Left, *bare-root rose before planting is completed.* Center, *how to cut back.* Right, *pruned and mounded with earth*

Bare-root plants should be soaked overnight, have their damaged roots cut off, and, after planting, be cut back to balance the loss of feeding roots. How much to cut is a matter of judgment. Usually, no more than six to eight inches is left above ground. Some experts recommend only three inches—the stronger shoots being left longer than the thin, weaker ones. The weakest ones are removed. Some enthusiasts also coat each cut with tree wound dressing, although with young, vigorous bushes this is rarely necessary. Much more important is to see that each stem ends with a bud pointing outward. This steers the new growth away from the center of the plant, letting in light for better growth and air to keep down diseases.

So far, we have treated all roses exactly alike. From here on, however, each rose is treated differently, according to type.

Hybrid Teas and Floribundas

These we shall take up first, because they are the most commonly grown of all roses. The hybrid teas are the large, individually flowered, ever-blooming type, such as Peace and President Herbert Hoover. The floribundas are somewhat similar but generally tend to be a little shorter and more cluster-flowered. Pinocchio and Fashion are examples.

The first thing to do is to remove all dead wood, cutting back to a good, strong, outward-pointing bud on live wood. Then take out all weak stems, twiggy growth, and stems showing canker scabs, making sure to cut at least an inch or an inch and a half below all signs of injury. Next look for suckers coming up from the roots. Follow this with the real pruning, which means shaping the plant and cutting back to produce good strong shoots for later bloom.

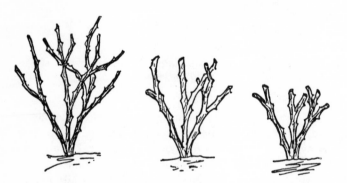

Left, *hybrid tea lightly pruned.* Center, *moderately cut.* Right, *cut back to live wood in cold climate*

For years we pruned roses by firm rules, each type cut back to a specific height. Now we do it by judgment, according to the strength of the plant. Also, we followed the rule that the harder we cut back, the stronger would be the resulting new stems. Now we know that there is much stored food in the stems, and that by leaving all the strong wood we can increase the size of the plants and the number and quality of the blooms, as well as the hardiness and life of the bushes. Where mildness of climate permits, try to cut the canes back to a diameter of half or three-eighths of an inch. This usually means a height of eighteen to twenty-four inches. Some enthusiasts may leave them much taller, and while this does produce many and good blooms it results in bushes five and six feet tall, much too high to be attractive or to display the flowers properly. Teas are handled in the same way. Roses to be used for exhibition blooms are cut back more severely than those intended for home use only.

Hybrid Perpetuals

These are the "monthly roses" of bygone days. In general, they are bigger, hardier bushes, less likely to freeze back but much less generous bloomers. Two of the best are Frau Karl Druschki, a good old white, still sold plentifully, and General Jacqueminot, the old red "Jack rose." These are handled much like the hybrid teas, except that since they are more cold-resistant, they need be cut back less in colder areas.

Shrub Roses

These are the old species and varieties that are still grown for their landscape value as shrubs and have only one blooming season. Two such are *Rosa hugonis,* or Father Hugo's rose, and Harrison's Yellow. Like shrubs they are merely trimmed a little here and there for shaping, and when they get old and leggy, one-fourth of the oldest canes are cut to the ground each year for four years to rejuvenate them.

Tree or Standard Roses

A rosebush on top of a tall bare stem is the best way to describe these. Being used for their landscape effect, as accents, the tall stems must never be cut. However, the grafted part on top of the stem or trunk requires similar but more severe pruning than the regular hybrid teas and floribundas, to keep them the proper size. First, remove weak or damaged portions and cut all the strong canes

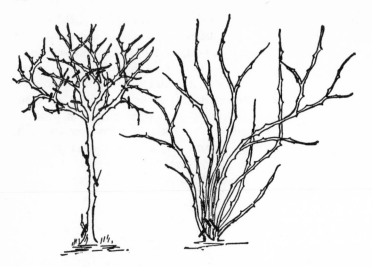

Left, *How to prune a tree rose.* Right, *pruning the rambler*

back to six to ten inches from where they come out of the trunk. Do all this at the end of the dormant season, just before new growth starts. Snip a little here and there during the growing season to keep them in shape, and also remove any sprouts along the stem and root suckers.

Miniatures

Like hybrid teas, these tiny roses should be banked for winter wherever severe cold prevails, and when spring comes, any dead or injured growth should be removed. Following this, whatever thinning, shaping, or other guiding seems necessary may be done. If they become very twiggy, they may be cut back almost to the ground and new tops allowed to grow.

The Ramblers

These are the old-style climbers. They usually flower but once a year and do best on stems produced the year before. A few are the old Dorothy Perkins, Crimson Rambler, and Paul's Scarlet Climber. Generally, they produce long canes and many smallish flowers in large clusters. The best way to handle them is to remove the old canes to the ground immediately after they have flowered. Fresh new ones soon grow in their place. These may be pinched or headed back as desired during the growing season, according to the size of the support upon which they are trained.

Large-flowered, Once-blooming Climbers

Generally, the large-flowered sorts do not produce as many canes as the rambler type. After blooming, the old flower clusters are best removed, leaving four to twelve inches of each lateral branch to flower next year. On well-established plants one or two of the oldest canes may be cut to the ground each year after flowering, to make room for vigorous young shoots.

Ever-blooming Climbers

These bloom again later in the season on the same canes and therefore should not be cut to the ground, except occasionally one or two of the oldest canes might be cut away to make room for strong new ones. Some are large-flowered—the climbing hybrid teas, teas, and polyanthas in the gentler climates. Others are cluster-roses like Blaze.

Left, *how to prune large-flowered climbers.* Center, *disbudding for better blooms.* Right, *cutting everblooming climbers*

About all the pruning they require is removal of the dead flowers, the cuts being made about a quarter-inch above the nearest leaf bud. Generally, the later flowers come from the buds hidden in the axils of these outermost leaves. Obviously, any wood injured or killed during winter should be removed in early spring. A little occasional shaping may also be practiced at this time, as well as the removal of any excess new shoots. Belle of Portugal, however, is an exception. It is so vigorous that at times a second summer cutting is needed.

Trailing Types

Those grown as trailers or ground covers usually need very little pruning. Dead wood, if any, is removed in early spring. After blooming, a little thinning is sometimes also in order. That is all.

REMOVING BLOOMS FOR CUT FLOWERS

Here inexperienced gardeners generally commit one or the other of two improper practices. They are either afraid to cut and take their flowers with stems too short to be useful or they scalp the poor plants, weakening them as a result.

The first year after planting the fewer blooms cut the better— if leaves are taken with the flowers. As the bushes grow stronger, cutting can become bolder. In any case, leave about a quarter-inch of stem above the leaf and be sure to leave not less than two well-developed leaves between the cut and where the branch joins the main stem. Only if long stems are really necessary is it advisable to cut back farther.

If too many flowers are being produced in a cluster or group, break out the excess buds as early as possible. For blooms of the finest quality it is also well to remove any axillary buds that may appear. By bending them over sharply they can usually be removed without leaving stubs, as is usually done when the buds are pinched out with the fingernails. Also, remove old flowers before they have had time to rob the plant by forming seed pods or hips.

When to cut the blooms for greatest lasting power is also important. For many years rosarians everywhere advocated cutting the flowers in early morning when the air is cool and the stems full of sap—and some still do. However, recent experiments by top-rank scientists have thrown this idea for a total loss. They found that cutting the blooms in the latter part of the afternoon, after the plants have had most of the day to manufacture food, gives them much greater lasting qualities.

SUCKERS

Once these were quite common. Now, thanks to better understocks and better positioning of the grafted buds, as well as more intelligent planting, they appear much less frequently. If suckers do start from below the graft they should be removed flush with the stem. But do not confuse suckers with basal shoots, which may also come from below ground but originate *above* the graft. Usually, you can tell by the leaves. True suckers generally have a perceptibly different foliage, although the old caution about removing everything that has more than five leaflets may be forgotten, because many modern roses will produce seven when growing vigorously.

TO INCREASE BLOOMING

While this is not strictly pruning, I have found this bit of advice helpful: If climbers either refuse to bloom or prove to be very shy, train the canes horizontally. This will often throw them into bloom when the proper season comes.

IX. The Small Fruits

The culture of small or bush fruits has increased rapidly in American gardens. However, their culture is not as well known as it should be for best results. Too often they are relegated to some out-of-the-way corner and left to fend for themselves. But given just a little attention, they will return the favor in a greatly increased crop of far better berries.

At planting time set them out as carefully as you would your choicest shrub. Give them a good soil, sun, and if they haven't already been cut back, reduce their height to one-third or one-fourth. This helps compensate for the loss of roots they suffered and gets them off to a better start. A little soluble fertilizer mixed with the water given them at this time also helps a lot.

Now for the individual plants:

Blackberries

Perhaps the easiest of all to grow, they are hardy, productive, and undemanding. Just as in the case of other bramble fruits that we shall discuss, upright blackberries produce roots that live indefinitely but the canes are biennial—they come up one year, fruit the next, and then die. They are vigorous growers and, unless well trained, soon make a solid mass of plants that is almost impossible to penetrate.

For best results the plants are set out in spring three to four feet apart and cut back to a short stub, as described above. Since they sucker freely, you have to decide early whether you want to grow them in hills, leaving three to five bearing canes per hill plus the same number of immature ones, or let them fill in the row, with the fruiting canes spaced six inches apart.

The first step in pruning is to remove all canes or suckers other than those you want. Here pulling out is better than cutting for it

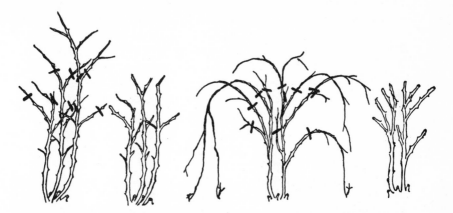

Left, *before and after pruning blackberry.* Right, *before and after cutting purple and black raspberries*

is less likely to promote additional sucker development. By mid-summer the canes will have shot up to a height of thirty to thirty-six inches. They should then be topped to prevent undue height that may tip the canes over. Topping will also encourage side growth.

The following spring, before growth commences, the laterals are cut back to twelve or six inches, depending upon the vigor of the plants. After fruiting, the old canes are cut to the ground. Should any diseased canes appear at any time, they are cut to the ground immediately and burned. Then wipe your knife or shears with alcohol to sterilize them.

Raspberries

These are divided into three distinct groups, the red, black, and purple-berried. Being the most common, we shall discuss the red first. In cold climates they are set out in early spring only, in the middle areas in early spring or during the fall. As with blackberries, the original canes are cut back but even more severely, sometimes to only a two- or three-inch stub.

There are three basic methods of culture: the hill system, linear row, and hedgerow. In the first method six to ten bearing stems are permitted every four to five feet apart and all suckers removed. In the linear row system, buds from the original crown are also used but the plants are set closer, eighteen to thirty-six inches in the East and thirty to forty in the West, where growth is more vigorous, and all suckers removed. In the hedgerow, plants are set out thirty-six inches apart and both crown buds and suckers are permitted to throw up canes in the row. Any suckers appearing between the rows are removed.

In the East, where the canes rarely grow much over five feet, only a light heading back is needed to make them stand up. On the West Coast, where the canes grow much longer, support is needed. Severe heading back is not recommended—most of the fruit is borne near the top of the stem and severe cutting would reduce the crop severely. Although natural laterals bear pretty well, artificially forced ones are seldom very productive.

When using the hill system tie the canes halfway up and at the top to six-foot stakes. In the linear row the canes are tied to one or two wires. Eastern growers sometimes train them on a pair of wires fastened to cross arms thirty inches from the ground and about a foot apart. In the hedgerow, since the canes are permitted to grow only five inches apart, they tend to hold one another up.

After fruiting, all the old canes should be removed to make room for the new ones. Weak or diseased ones are also removed at this time. Everbearing varieties such as Indian Summer, Durham, and September bear a few fruits at tips the first summer and the main crop on the same canes the following one. So, do not prune any tips until after fruiting.

The black and purple raspberries do not sucker appreciably, but produce bearing laterals more freely than the red. Therefore, when they are two or two and a half feet tall, head them back at once. The following winter head the laterals back to six or three inches, according to the strength of the cane, to improve the fruit quality. Black and purple raspberries are grown primarily by the hill system and in the Far West wire support is usually given. As with the reds, old, weak, and diseased canes are removed immediately after fruiting.

Dew-, Young-, Boysen-, Nectar-, and Loganberries

These are all improved forms of the trailing blackberry. In the Northeast they are inclined to be somewhat tender but they are widely grown in the milder climates of the Far West. Because of their vigorous growth, they are usually trained on posts or wires. Like the others, the canes last only two years and should be removed promptly after fruiting.

If they are grown unsupported, the canes are tipped at two to three feet in summer and the laterals cut back the following spring to about a foot. When fanned out on a trellis the shoots are usually headed back at five to six feet and the laterals handled as above. Sometimes the canes are not tipped but draped over a wire trellis. While more fruit is produced this way, it is generally of inferior quality.

Himalayan Blackberry

This sort makes tremendous canes, up to forty feet long in one season. The laterals do not form until the second year and bear for several years. Four canes are usually enough for each plant. Train horizontally on a permanent trellis, pinch out tips when they reach the desired length, and later head in the laterals as above. Remove all suckers but let the canes bear three or four years. New canes for replacement are generally grown along the ground beneath the plants until they are needed to replace old canes that have been removed.

Currants

Currants are more popular in colder areas than warm and are usually trained as many-stemmed shrubs. Plants are usually set out very early in the spring and cut back to two or three strong canes. Several strong shoots develop. The weaker ones are removed and those left are headed back slightly in late winter. The second season they bear some fruit and develop spurs as well as new shoots from the base.

Both red and white currants develop fruit buds at the base of year-old wood and on spurs on older wood. Therefore, as maturity is reached remove any canes that are weak or infested with borers.

Before and after cutting currant and gooseberries

Then thin the remainder to two to four three-year canes, three to five two-year canes, and four to six one-year canes, to provide a good selection from which to choose later.

Black currants bear most of their fruit on one-year canes. Therefore, very little old wood should be retained. Each winter remove the weakest canes and all more than a year old. Thin the remainder and shorten by a quarter the six to ten strongest ones left.

Gooseberries

Prune these much the same as currants, but note that they bear both on new shoots and on spurs on the older wood. Growth is usually thick, so in late winter thin out the new canes and remove all canes over three years old back to renewal shoots near their bases, or back to three- or two-inch stubs to force out shoots.

Blueberries

Of the three types we shall discuss the low-bush species first. These are almost always wild plants growing over large areas. Hand pruning is generally impractical. Hay (one ton per acre) is spread over the plants, allowed to pack down to the ground, and then set afire when plants and hay are dry but the ground is frozen or wet. This eliminates competing growth and promotes both root spread and the development of strong upright shoots. These shoots then bear a heavy crop of fruit buds the first year, less the second, and few the third, meaning another burning is in order.

High-bush blueberries are the mainstay of the group but they tend to bear too much. Pruning must be kept up for best results. Since the berries are borne on year-old wood, a continuous supply must be kept coming. Varieties may vary widely. The old Rubel is upright while others may spread.

When set out, bushes are usually two years old. At first, only two or three strong shoots are permitted and weak side shoots removed as well as fruit buds. The second year after planting a few berries may be permitted but weak stems are removed and any that have not grown at least six inches.

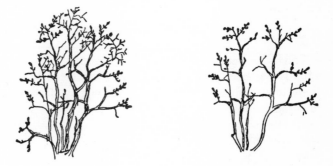

Before and after severe pruning of highbush blueberry

On mature bushes (four years or more after planting) all weak shoots must come out, as well as branches too close to the ground and a few of the oldest stems. After that, thin the younger ones as necessary. Also remove tired twiggy branches in the tops. Some, such as Pioneer, Scammell, and Cabot, benefit from heading back the fruiting terminals to get better fruit. Concord, Stanley, Jersey, Rubel, Rancocas, June, and Weymouth do not, but Concord, Rancocas, and Rubel need some thinning out of small branches within the bush. In milder climates pruning can begin in early winter. In severe ones wait until early spring.

Rabbit-Eye blueberries, a southern type, grow much like the high-bush. Remove the oldest stems and thin out small, weak and twiggy growth, but try to prune lightly to prevent reducing the crop too severely without corresponding gain in fruit size.

Elderberries

Although there are several species of elderberries growing wild in this country, there are very few cultivated varieties. One is Adams, introduced in New York State. For the most part elderberries are large, coarse shrubs or small trees with rather thick, pithy stems not adapted too much to cutting. However, elderberries rarely need pruning, except to thin out stems occasionally and to rejuvenate from time to time by cutting back some of the oldest stems to the ground in late winter. In some Midwestern states elderberries appear to grow and produce well if they are cut to the ground each year.

High-bush Cranberry

This is not cranberry at all but the native *Viburnum trilobum,* a hardy northern fruit growing into a shrub ten to twelve feet high. If the bushes become too thick, thin out as circumstances indicate to permit new growth.

Dwarf Cherries

These include the sand, Nanking, and Korean cherries, bushy shrubs from three to eight feet tall. They need little attention except removal of dead stems and thinning if they become too thick. If in really bad condition, they can be rejuvenated by cutting almost to the ground and growing new tops.

Strawberries

These are not woody plants and therefore are not pruned in the usual sense. We include them merely to round out the treatment of small fruits.

Except for a few nonspreading sorts such as the Baron Solemacher, strawberries increase by throwing out runners that root and make new plants, the process continuing indefinitely. If you want to grow them in solid beds by the matted row system, leave the runners on. If you prefer the hill system, take them off as soon as they appear. If you want new plants to replace the old, tired ones, let the desired number of runners develop and form new plants. When sufficiently strong either move them to a new location or leave them and turn the old plants under by plowing or spading.

X. Large Ornamental Trees

Now we are getting into a real man's job, for, while the pruning of large flowering and shade trees is not in itself difficult, getting up into the tree sometimes is. Before we get too far into the subject it seems advisable to offer this piece of advice: Don't tackle the pruning of a large tree unless you are positive you have the right equipment and can take care of yourself off the ground. If there is any doubt in your mind, hire a competent tree man to do your work for you. Make sure he is a true arborist. A tree butcher—and there are some—can cause damage that can never be repaired.

WHY PRUNE LARGE TREES?

Large trees, like smaller ones, need care. They sometimes need a little guidance to maintain proper form. Dead or broken branches must be removed before they fall and cause harm to persons or property. Diseased tissue must be removed before it spreads to healthy. Low-hanging branches may present obstructions, high ones may be endangering windows or roof, others may be rubbing and causing injury to the tree itself.

WHEN TO PRUNE

There is flexibility here. In cold climates the best time is late winter or very early spring before growth starts, for then large wounds heal noticeably better. However, most trees can be pruned successfully practically all year round.

Of course there are some exceptions. Maples, birches, yellowwoods, and walnuts, bleed severely. While the process is rarely severe enough to cause irreparable injury, it is a nuisance and may permit disease to get a foothold. Thus, maples and such are better pruned in summer, when the sap flow is less vigorous. Also, in warm climates where there is a moist season and a dry season, pruning is best done just as the plants are coming out of their rest season and about to commence growth. Finally, where large, showy flowers are concerned, it is usually advisable to postpone pruning until after flowering is past.

HOW TO PRUNE

We have already discussed the mechanics of pruning. As a general reminder, remember to cut each branch as close to the trunk or crotch as possible; leave no stubs or points that may interfere with healing and let decay enter; do not butcher trees back or make ugly holes through them for wires; avoid stripping down the bark; trim all large wounds to elliptical shapes wherever possible and leave neat edges to promote healing; eliminate crisscrossing branches; remove water sprouts and, in most cases, stump sprouts.

Some Exceptions

No matter what we say, there are always some special cases. For instance, the needle-leaved evergreens, whose problems we have already covered in Chapter VI. Now for a few more.

On the West Coast many thousands of eucalyptus trees grow, some by human choice, others not. They all have one weakness. They grow long, seemingly strong branches that go through the severest storms and then suddenly, for no apparent reason, drop. Watch out, if you ever try to climb them! As a precaution the branches are often cut back to stubs, leaving the trees looking like telegraph poles with feather dusters attached. With this particular tree complete loss seldom occurs. Just thin out the surplus branches, leaving the strongest ones to carry on.

Deciduous magnolias can often seem to harden their trunks and restrict sap flow. When this happens annual growth becomes stunted and strong suckers may appear. Suckers coming from below the connection on grafted trees should be removed at once. If they appear above the graft they may be left eventually to replace the parent trunk when it becomes too stunted.

Subtropical trees, because they are out of their original environment, sometimes get too shrubby. The only cure is to remove the lower branches, thin heavily, head back the side branches but *not* the leader, and feed and water generously. This will usually throw them back into treelike form.

SPECIAL PROBLEMS

Although most of the following matters are best handled by professional tree men, there are times and places when the home owner is forced to take care of them himself. Obviously, he should do so only with the utmost care.

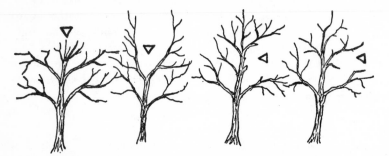

Three wrongs and one right way to provide clearance for wires. Left to right, beheading, deep crotching, the big hole method, judicious directional pruning

Keeping power or telephone wires in the clear is done in one of four ways, the *first three* of which are *not recommended:* (1) The whole top of the tree is taken off to prevent its contact with the overhead wires. (2) Large branches are removed to create a hole on the side of the tree to let the wires through. (3) Large center portions are cut back to outward-pointing laterals. Known as deep-crotching, the method is little better than the first two. (4) Just enough small branches are removed to let the wires through inconspicuously, and the neighboring branches are tailored just enough to guide future growth away from the trouble area. This technique is known as directional pruning.

At no time should branches be allowed to lie on or rub against a roof, for they will cause serious harm one way or another. Instead of stubbing the offending branch just beyond the roof's edge, use a pole pruner or saw to cut off all smaller, downward-pointing branches (flush with the main branch, of course). The reduction of weight usually permits the main branch to rise harmlessly off the roof. Now shape the neighboring branches back as necessary to keep the tree's shape natural.

Left, *wrong way to cut a branch rubbing on roof.* Right, *correct way*

When a tree appears to be starving in the midst of plenty, it may be suffering from root girdling or self-strangulation due to faulty planting. For years the tree does well but as the trunk and roots increase in diameter the strangulation gradually takes place. The cure: dig down around the trunk. If you uncover strangling roots, saw them through, taking out the entire section, cover the cuts with tree paint, and return the soil. Recovery will not be fast but a good feeding out where the root tips are will help.

This seems a good place to describe "jump cutting," since it is a useful trick for high work in shade trees. First, the limb is sawed about a third or half through from the underside. Then another cut is made on the top surface one to two inches *out beyond* the first one. When the upper cut reaches the level of the lower one, the wood between breaks off cleanly and the severed limb jumps away from the cutting area. Thus, this is a handy way to drop a branch without lowering it by means of a rope, provided there is room enough for it to fall without damaging tree or property. If possible, follow up with a smooth, clean cut farther back.

WHAT ABOUT WOODLAND TREES?

To some gardeners this is a minor issue but with the increasing penetration of suburbs into wooded areas many new home owners find they wish to retain at least a small portion of the original woodland in a natural state. Basically, this means cutting as little as possible. However, dead trees should be removed. Diseased trees or branches should be removed and burned to prevent spread of the trouble. Broken branches should be removed close to the parent branch or trunk. Trees or branches that are shading such desirable understory material as flowering dogwoods, redbuds, hollies, and the like are candidates for removal. Likewise, if an undergrowth of shrubs or a new generation of young tree seedlings is desired, a similar thinning of trees and branches is advisable.

If timber is the object, then it is desirable to remove the lowest branches periodically, as soon as they could be spared, to produce good clean boles (trunks) with as few knots as possible. Growth will be stimulated by the removal of unprofitable species and cripples and will let in sunlight.

CABLING AND BRACING

Never place naked guy wires around a tree trunk to hold it up. Run them through short pieces of old garden hose to prevent rubbing or girdling. Where permanent guy wires are necessary an extra loop of cable may be placed around the tree over a series of short slats encircling the trunk.

Crotches or limbs that need support to prevent breakage should not be wrapped with chains or cables. Either place large screw

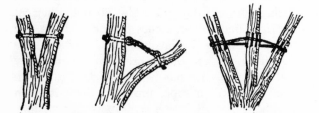

Methods of supporting limbs. Left to right, *tie-bolt, eye-bolts and cable, three-way cable brace*

eyes into each and then fasten together with cable or chain or run a large eyebolt right through each branch and handle in the same way. Occasionally, one large tie bolt or rod can be run right through both branches.

FEEDING—WHEN, WHERE, AND HOW

While not exactly pruning, pruning and feeding often go hand in hand in tree care. As a rule, people do not stop to think that trees need occasional feedings. True, sometimes they don't, but if growth is slow or the tree looks weak and hungry, feed it. In general, the best time is early spring although some tree men also like to feed in fall to stimulate root growth while the top is inactive. If the tree is obviously starving, feeding any time but in late summer is better than waiting.

A common mistake is to put the fertilizer too close to the trunk. This does no good whatever. The feeding roots are out from the trunk approximately as far as the tips of the branches. The outer two-thirds of the branch spread and about half that distance beyond is the proper area. Put the fertilizer in crowbar holes spaced about two feet apart and run eighteen inches to two feet deep. Water then, and fill the holes to the surface with good soil, unless you don't mind the holes showing for a while.

Trees six inches or less in diameter—diameters are calculated at breast height, or four feet from the ground—feed at the rate of two to three pounds for every inch of diameter. Larger trees should get three to five pounds per inch.

As for the kind of food to use, there are almost as many formulas as there are tree experts. A safe rule to follow is to use any good balanced fertilizer recommended in your area for roses, shrubs, or root vegetables. However, if your tree very obviously needs a good stiff shot in the arm, it is sometimes preferable to substitute a balanced fertilizer high in nitrogen, such as that normally sold for lawns.

ROAD MAP TO PRUNING TREES—BY KINDS

Although a few exceptions will be found, the trees discussed here are primarily ornamental ones, either shade or flowering. Also included are some broad-leaved evergreens that grow in milder areas.

For the needle-leaved types, however, see Chapter VI. Because the boundary lines between shrubs and trees is indistinct, some trees were treated with shrubs in Chapter V. Fruit and nut trees will be discussed in Chapters XI and XII respectively.

Where no care is mentioned in the following descriptions, the only pruning needed is slight guidance. The figures in parenthesis refer in every case to height.

Acer—Maple
FORM: Round, spreading.
USES: Streets. A little dense for lawns.
CARE: Need little except to open up if lawns suffer from shade. Bleed; prune summer or fall.

Aesculus—Horse Chestnut
FORM: Tall, broad pyramid.
USES: Streets, large plantings.
CARE: Tree inclined to be messy but needs little pruning.

Ailanthus—Tree of Heaven
FORM: Flat-topped, very open, tropical-looking.
USES: Hardiest of all in crowded cities.
CARE: Needs some guidance. Remove suckers.

Albizzia—Hardy Mimosa
FORM: Small, broad (36′). Fine-cut leaves.
USES: Ornamental flowers, June–August. Pink form hardy to Boston.

Betula—Birch
FORM: Open, slender.
USES: Lawn specimens, border plantings, woodlands.
CARE: Bleed. Prune summer or fall to prevent narrow crotches and shape tree.

Carpinus—Hornbeam, Ironwood
FORM: Small, shrubby (30′). Sinewy trunks. Very hard wood.
USES: lawns, copses near water, hedges.
CARE: Stands severe cutting, if desired.

Castanea—Chestnut (hybrid Orientals)
FORM: Mostly broad, smallish trees available (American not considered).
USES: Lawns, woods edges, orchards.
CARE: Remove blighted parts completely, if appear.

Catalpa—Indian Bean, Cigar tree
FORM: Broad, open, round head, spreading (45–60′). Large leaves.
USES: Lawns, dooryards. Showy blooms, June–July.

Celtis—Hackberry
FORM: Tall, thinnish, sometimes vaselike (120′).
USES: General use, streets, near shore.
CARE: Often develops witches'-broom, which remove. Train.

Ceratonia—**Carob,**
   St.-John's-Bread
FORM: Smallish, rounded (40').
USES: Sometimes grown for edible pods. Stands dry soil. Only warmest parts U.S. (Florida and Southern California).

Cercidiphyllum—**Katsura Tree**
FORM: Broad, spreading, often branches low, neat (80–90').
USES: Specimens, street tree if headed up.

Cercis—**Redbud**
FORM: Irregular, flat-topped, vase-like, small (35').
USES: Pinkish, pealike flowers before leaves. Ornamental plantings, specimens.
CARE: Prune after flowering to shape.

Chionanthus—**Fringe Tree**
FORM: Shrubby to small (30').
USES: Whitish flowers, June. Ornament.
CARE: Late to leaf out. Do not mistake for dead. Cut after flowers.

Cladrastis—**Yellowwood**
FORM: Broad, rounded (50').
USES: Lawns, backgrounds. White flowers a little like wisteria, June.
CARE: Prune after flowering.

Cornus—**Flowering Dogwood**
FORM: Handsome, small, tallish (40'). Horizontal branches.
USES: U.S. type blooms before leaves, Oriental, after.
CARE: Heals slowly. Do not cut large branches needlessly.

Cocos—**Coconut** .
FORM: Tall, slender, graceful.
USES: Shade and ornament, warmest regions.
CARE: Do not try to cut off like a northern tree.

Crataegus—**Hawthorn**
FORM: Smallish, broad, like apple (20–35'). Many kinds.
USES: Grown for flowers.
CARE: Prune like apple tree, if needed.

Davidia—**Dove Tree**
FORM: Straight, upright branches, open habit (60').
USES: Showy 7-inch flowers, May. For large areas.
CARE: Not reliable bloomer north of Long Island, N.Y.

Delonix—**Royal Poinciana**
FORM: Open, wide-branching (40').
USES: Flowers in summer, south Florida.
CARE: As needed, after bulk of flowering.

Elaeagnus—**Russian Olive**
FORM: Wide-spreading, open (20').
USES: Ornaments, windbreaks, backgrounds. Especially useful on cold northern plains.

Eriobotrya—**Loquat**
FORM: Neat, rounded, compact.
USES: Specimens, for fruit.
CARE: Thin out, if too dense, in fall. If for fruit, remove half of each flower cluster.

Eucalyptus—**Eucalyptus**
FORM: Tall, spreading, weak; rapid grower.

USES: Specimens not too close to house.
CARE: Spring or after blooming. Drops branches. Head them back occasionally. Sprouts even from stump.

Fagus—**Beech**
FORM: Large, dense, broad (90').
USES: Shade, streets, lawns, hedges, espaliers.

Franklinia—**Franklinia**
FORM: Upright, small (30').
USES: Large white flowers, summer.
CARE: Prune early spring.

Fraxinus—**Ash**
FORM: Erect, usually round-headed (60–120').
USES: Streets, shade over house, etc.

Ginkgo—**Ginkgo, Maidenhair Tree**
FORM: Tall, pyramidal when young, irregularly spreading later (120').
USES: City streets, parks, lawns, etc.
CARE: Use only males, fruits messy.

Gleditsia—**Honey Locust**
FORM: Tall, open-headed, loose, sometimes elmlike (125'). Has character.
USES: High, light shade. Streets, homes.

Gordonia—**Franklinia**
FORM: Shrub or small tree (30').
USES: Specimen for flowers in summer. Hardy to Philadelphia.

Gordonia—**Loblolly Bay**
FORM: Narrow-headed, dense (60').
USES: For shade, white flowers in summer. North to Virginia.

Gymnocladus—**Kentucky Coffee Tree**
FORM: Tall, narrow-headed (80'). Stout branches, several leaders.
USES: For winter character. Likes deep, rich soil.

Halesia—**Carolina Silverbell**
FORM: Small, somewhat round-headed (30').
USES: Spring flowers, specimens, woodlands.
CARE: If necessary, after blooming.

Harpullia—**Harpullia**
FORM: Rounded, dense.
USES: Specimens, general plantings.
CARE: Clean up, thin in spring.

Hicoria—**Hickory**
FORM: Shagbark narrow (70'); pecan broader (125').
USES: Good for winter character. Light shade. Nuts.
CARE: Summer sometimes preferred to early spring.

Hoheria—**Hoheria**
FORM: Upright; drooping branches.
USES: Specimens, clumps.
CARE: After flowering. Train to single stem or many stems.

Jacaranda—**Jacaranda**
FORM: Fine-leaved, round-headed (40').
USES: Specimens, street trees, general use. Warm climates.
CARE: Remove small inner branches that die back. Any time.

Juglans—**Walnut**
FORM: Broad, spreading (60–140'). Heavy but open-branched.

USES: Shade and nuts.
CARE: Bleed. Prune early summer.

*Koelreuteria—***Goldenrain Tree**
FORM: Open, flat-topped (30').
USES: Specimens for blooms in early summer.
CARE: Neater with spent flowers removed.

*Laburnum—***Golden Chain**
FORM: Stiffly upright or vaselike, willowy branches.
USES: Specimens for flowers, wall planting.
CARE: Light shaping after blooming.

*Leucadendron—***Silver Leucadendron**
FORM: Attractive, rounded, short-lived (35').
USES: Gardens, streets.

*Liquidambar—***Sweet Gum**
FORM: Broad, pyramidal (125').
USES: Specimens, streets, home shade.
CARE: Keep to one strong leader when young.

*Liriodendron—***Tulip Tree**
FORM: Tall, straight-trunked, high-branched (150').
USES: Streets, parks, high shade over house.

*Maclura—***Osage Orange**
FORM: Open, irregular, thorny, round top (60').
USES: Hedges, fence rows, windbreaks.
CARE: Stands hard cutting.

*Magnolia—***Magnolia**
FORM: Small to large (20–150'). Often open, irregular.
USES: Specimens, backgrounds, shade, espaliers. For flowers.
CARE: Prune early summer, little as possible. Remove suckers. If top is stunted, replace with strongest sucker above graft. Evergreen type: thin young plants to build framework. Cut for decoration any time—bud well from old wood.

*Malus—***Crab Apple**
FORM: Usually small, broad-headed (10–35').
USES: Specimens for flowers, fruit, shade, landscape form.
CARE: Same as fruit apples.

*Maytenus—***Chile Mayten**
FORM: Upright, branches arching or pendulous.
USES: Clumps, specimens, streets and parks, seashores.
CARE: Remove suckers unless clump wanted. Stands heavy shaping.

*Melia—***Umbrella Tree, Chinaberry**
FORM: Round-headed, compact, dense (45').
USES: Streets, specimens, shade.

*Myoporum—***Myoporum**
FORM: Rounded.
USES: Windbreaks, specimens.
CARE: Remove weak and dead wood, frozen parts. Stands severe cutting back, producing growth from wood any age.

Nyssa—**Sourgum, Tupelo**
FORM: Broad, flat-topped, with horizontal or drooping branches (60').
USES: Specimens for winter form, scarlet leaves, especially in wet places.

Oxydendrum—**Sourwood**
FORM: Narrow pyramid (20–70').
USES: Shade, specimens, background for shrubs.

Paulownia—**Empress Tree**
FORM: Round-headed, with stout branches (50').
USES: Shade, specimens for flowers.
CARE: In North may need removal of frozen branches in spring.

Phellodendron—**Cork Tree**
FORM: Low-branching, broad, open, with heavy corky bark and branches (45').
USES: Shade, streets, winter interest.

Phoenix—**Date Palm**
FORM: Rounded top on graceful trunk (30').
USES: Streets, specimens.
CARE: Trim off old foliage as necessary. Do not cut trunk.

Platanus—**Plane Tree**
FORM: Large, broad-headed (90').
USES: Streets, shade over houses, large-scale plantings.

Populus—**Poplar, Cottonwood, Aspen**
FORM: Mostly large, open-branched pyramids (50–150').
USES: Shade, streets, windbreaks.
CARE: Soft, brittle, easily broken by wind. Prune as needed.

Prunus—**Flowering Cherries, Plums, etc.**
FORM: Mostly small, broad.
USES: Specimens, primarily for spring blooms.
CARE: Prune only after flowering for correction. Remove frost damage in cold climates. Spring.

Pterostyrax—**Epaulet Tree**
FORM: Open-headed; slender, spreading branches (45').
USES: Specimens for bloom, late spring.
CARE: Guide to form when young, remove suckers. Tender when young. Remove frost damage in spring.

Quercus—**Oak**
FORM: Usually large, upright, broad-headed, sturdy.
USES: Shade and streets, clipped hedges, and screens.
CARE: Both deciduous and evergreen types stand hard pruning if desired. Fall.

Rhus—**Sumac**
FORM: Small, open, with coarse branches (15–35').
USES: Naturalistic plantings. Smoketree as specimen.
CARE: Guide as needed. Wood brittle, repair damage.

Robinia—**Black Locust**
FORM: Tall, slender, open-branched (75').
USES: Light shade, winter character, flowers in spring.
CARE: Brittle, repair as needed. Remove suckers. Can be kept to

broad, dense hedge by cutting after blooming.

*Roystonea—***Royal Palm**
FORM: Graceful (70').
USES: Specimens, streets, parks.
CARE: Give light clean-up periodically to keep neat. Do not cut trunk.

*Sabal palmetto—***Palmetto**
FORM: Tuft of large leaves atop tall trunk (90').
USES: Shade, general ornament. One of hardiest palms. The buds may be eaten but plant dies.
CARE: Clean up as necessary.

*Salix—***Willow**
FORM: Large or small; upright except weeping willow.
USES: Specimens, clumps, natural plantings, screens and hedges, shade.
CARE: Brittle, easily broken. Repair as needed after taking pussies. Guide when young. Remove suckers. Can be cut very hard.

*Sassafras—***Sassafras**
FORM: Tall, slender, sparse-branched (60').
USES: Hedgerows, shade, natural groups.
CARE: Brittle. Guide when young, trim as needed. Remove suckers.

*Schinus—***Pepper Tree**
FORM: Round-headed. Spreading, pendant branches (40').
USES: Streets, specimens, shade.

*Sophora—***Pagoda, Scholar Tree**
FORM: Spreading, round-headed (70').
USES: Streets and lawns.
CARE: Train while young, clean up after bloom.

*Sorbus—***Mountain Ash**
FORM: Usually erect, not too broad (30–45').
USES: Specimens for berries in fall.
CARE: Guidance and damage-repair only. Spring.

*Sterculia—***Bottle Tree**
FORM: Sturdy, round-headed (60').
USES: Shade and streets.

*Stewartia—***Stewartia**
FORM: Rounded, can be bushy (10–60').
USES: Specimens — camellia-like flowers in summer.
CARE: Guide while young. Early spring, especially in North.

*Tilia—***Linden**
FORM: Dense, rounded or pyramidal (60–100').
USES: Shade, streets, parks.
CARE: If grafted, needs guidance to grow upright while young. Bark heals quickly after cutting.

*Ulmus—***Elm**
FORM: Open, graceful. Vase form most pronounced in America (50–120').
USES: Shade, streets.
CARE: Remove any diseased parts at once.

Umbellularia—**California Bay, Pepperwood**
FORM: Rounded, compact.
USES: Specimen, hedge, tub plant.
CARE: Prune for shape, even severely. Can stump sprout in spring or summer.

Zelkova—**Zelkova**
FORM: Short-trunked, round-topped, with upreaching branches (90'). More like American elm than any other tree.
USES: Shade, specimens, streets.

XI. How to Handle Fruit Trees

In Chapter IV we discussed the training of the young tree. Now, we take it from there.

What we have just written about shade trees applies also to fruit trees—except that they seldom get so tall and are less likely to be planted where they conflict with buildings and overhead wires. However, the fruiting process gives us a few added factors to consider. Pruning, for instance, must be done every year, for best results. Unless otherwise indicated in the following discussions, it is assumed that you will prune during the dormant or least active season.

GARDEN VERSUS ORCHARD PRUNING

"Just do what the orchard man does," you are likely to hear if you are one of the many new home owners faced with pruning for the first time. But, there are some basic differences. He is interested in only one thing: the greatest possible production of top-quality fruit at the lowest possible cost. He trains his branches low, sometimes barely above the ground, and keeps the crown as low as possible to facilitate pruning, spraying, and picking. The mere appearance of his tree is a secondary consideration.

To the home gardener, on the other hand, the appearance may easily be more important than the fruit. Therefore he heads his tree high enough for him to be able to walk under it. Likewise, he often sacrifices some of his fruit production by eliminating bearing branches and fruiting spurs to get an attractive, clean-limbed, open center.

BASIC SYSTEMS OF TRAINING

There are three systems of training. The first is the central leader system. This is the most like that used in training ornamental trees. It is based on one central or main trunk with all other growth subservient. Because of the difficulty of working taller trees and the tendency to shade the lower parts the system has pretty well gone out in orchards, except in the cases of some nuts (as we shall note later) and some tropical fruits. In home gardens, however, it still has some use, as it usually produces a more attractively shaped tree that is also a little less subject to breakage in snow and ice.

The modified leader is a more widely recommended system. In Chapter IV we selected the main or scaffold branches. Here it is necessary to remember that branches never change their height. If you start them at three feet, there they will remain. So, get them started where you want them! The branches of sweet cherries, pears, and some plums aim sharply upward at a very close angle, while those of apples, peaches, and prunes may tend to sprawl, hence these latter must be started higher. The method is the same

Left to right, *tree with central leader, modified leader, open center*

as in the central leader system, but in addition to the leader you also select a few other branches—usually the two lowest—for almost equal importance, removing all others or heading them back to become secondaries.

The third system is the open-center tree. This is now relatively little used, except for peaches, nectarines, sour cherries, and pecans and almonds among the nuts. All the scaffold branches are selected at one time and made to branch out from the trunk at about the same height. This produces a more or less goblet-shaped tree, more easily damaged by wind and ice, which may strip the branches down or cause pockets where water collects and rot sets in.

A delayed open center is better. Some branches are started early, as in the modified leader, and then two or three caused to grow out at a higher point by heading back the leader a little higher up. The result is more like the modified-leader tree and the branches are better spaced out than in the straight open-center method.

Of course, we still follow the basic rules of pruning: We thin out to let sun in to ripen the fruit. We remove all branches that rub against or shade others. We remove all suckers and water sprouts. We remove all damaged, dying, or diseased wood. We also remove some branches in a little moderate thinning to improve the quality of the fruit.

HOW TO REJUVENATE OLD TREES

Coupled with a good feeding of high-nitrogen fertilizer in early spring, pruning can often reinvigorate long-neglected trees. With apples and pears, the first year remove all broken and diseased wood, water sprouts, and all upright and crowded branches. This should bring on a surge of growth that will show you which are the vigorous branches to keep, which the tired old ones to remove the second winter. If the tree is too tall, head back a few branches severely each year to reshape and get all growth within easy reach. Since no two neglected trees are in quite the same state, it is not possible to give further specific instructions. Use your judgment but do not be afraid to cut. It is important to encourage strong new shoots. Then thin out wherever too thick.

Peaches, plums, and cherries, too, can be rejuvenated in some measure although of all the group peaches are the shortest lived. Again, feed. Head back into the original scaffold limbs. Most will send out new shoots all over. Select the ones you want the following spring and thin out the rest to develop a new set of bearing laterals. Any branches too old to respond should be removed completely and new shoots allowed to take their place.

With all these trees the drastic, one-step dehorning of the past is now out of date. The shock to the tree is not so great with the newer methods and the intervening complete loss of crops is eliminated.

THE FRUITS INDIVIDUALLY CONSIDERED

Apple

Apples tend to grow widespread, so the modified leader or central leader system is used. The first few years the tree is encouraged to grow upright to space the branches out. Scaffold branches may number from only three to as many as eight, arranged in somewhat of a spiral around the trunk and eight to twelve inches apart. Then fruiting begins.

The next five to ten years' pruning to keep the tree open becomes steadily more important. The scaffold branches are maintained and as the new growth on the branches shortens, some must be removed to prevent crowding. In other words, as the tree gets older and bears heavier crops, shoot growth decreases in length—from two feet a year to six inches in the case of a McIntosh.

As the branches bear increasingly larger loads of fruit the weight gradually forces them from upright to drooping. Growth slows, and fruit quality suffers. At this point the drooping part should be removed back to the nearest almost-vertical shoot and the process started all over again.

An important thing to bear in mind is the manner in which apples fruit. The apple produces both simple leaf buds and compound buds—buds containing both leaves and flowers. These fruit-bearing buds grow at the ends of short spurs and, to a smaller extent, on branch terminals. The spurs are generally produced on two- to four-year wood and have a life span of ten years or more, although after the first few years their rate of production drops. Therefore, sufficient new growth must be maintained by feeding and proper pruning to ensure replacement. Varieties that bear mostly on spurs tend toward producing a good crop every second year. Examples are the Baldwin, Wealthy, York Imperial. Those that bear more on the young shoots generally are steadier bearers—the Delicious group, McIntosh, and Rome Beauty.

Apricot

In its bearing habits the apricot both resembles and differs from the peach. Both produce simple buds that may develop in threes: two flower buds and one leaf bud in the axil of the previous year's leaf. Though the peach produces a few fruits on short growths on the older stems, these are hardly true spurs and do not continue growth. The apricot, however, produces a large part of its crop on spurs that last three to four years. However, by this time the branches should be removed and replaced with younger ones.

In general, the apricot is pruned fairly heavily. It is usually a strong grower and heavy bearer and unless checked will bear its fruit too high. Usually it is trained to a modified leader. When bearing age is reached it is usually thinned and headed back one-third to one-half of the new growth each year. Long, thin branches are not allowed and the tree takes on a stubby look. In the warm inland valleys a little more growth is left for shading.

Commercial growers usually remove about one-third or one-quarter of the older lateral branches each year. Home gardeners can be more lenient, if they wish.

Avocado

These are beautiful specimen trees, worth growing for appearance alone. Seedling trees are usually worthless for fruit. Grafted ones are more bushy and compact. To avoid storm damage and aid handling, head low and then let grow naturally. Trim out weak and improperly placed branches and head back again if they persist in growing upward at the expense of the laterals. Carefully paint all wounds and do not open up too much. The thin bark sunburns easily.

Calamondin

Treat same as orange.

Cherry

Sweet cherries tend to grow tall and upright with stiff, narrow branching; sour cherries are more spreading. The treatment differs.

For the sweet cherry, use the modified leader system. On young trees head the upright shoots back to outward-pointing laterals—or, if necessary, to where you want laterals to form. This gets spread into the framework. Then thin out unwanted shoots. Summer pinching the first few years is helpful in that it causes branching without leaving stubs to die back. Prune gently, especially while young, to encourage as many fruiting spurs as possible on the branches. Keep out any strong shoots that would compete with the leader. Later, cut back into two- and three-year wood occasionally to renew the spur-bearing branches—but never more than ten per cent at one time. Prune mostly for training. Unlike many fruits, cherries color well even in shade.

Sour cherries make a more irregular, broad-headed tree. Hence, train by the delayed open-center system, removing the droopy laterals to force the growth upright. Prune a little heavier than on the sweet cherry but still with caution. Some growers prefer to cut heavily every six to ten years. A moderate opening up keeps the spurs active longer. With both sweet and sour, winter injury often occurs on the southwest side of the trunk. So, try to start a branch fairly low to protect this area.

Crab Apple

Treat same as apple.

Date

Unlike most fruits, the date palm has only one terminal bud. Consequently, this cannot be touched without harm to the tree. Thus, if any get too tall, the only cure is to start new trees. Some of the lower leaves may be removed to thin, to improve pollination, and to help picking, but enough leaves must be left to shade the fruit from direct sunlight. Although the size of the fruit appears to be in direct proportion to the number of leaves, some California growers recommended reducing the number of leaves to one hundred and twenty per tree in June.

Fig

Figs differ considerably in their manner of growth and so do the methods of pruning them. The Calimyrna does not produce laterals unless it is forced to. Prune heavily while young to produce a satisfactory framework and a properly balanced tree. Once the tree reaches bearing age, little pruning is needed unless it becomes too rank. Then, head back and thin out as needed.

California Black, or Mission, and Adriatic figs make large shrubs with plenty of low, spreading branches. Cut back when planting and select the scaffold branches in the first dormant pruning. Do not head back the primary branches. Fruit is borne on the new wood, which is produced freely enough without forcing it. On bearing trees prune tops only if branches die, rub, or get in the way.

Kadota figs are vigorous and are often headed low to produce spreading, flat-topped trees. This is done by heading the growth harder near the center of the tree than around the edges. New growth is headed back twelve to eighteen inches each year.

Handle Capri figs the same way but since their growth is less vigorous, cut back less. Tip pruning, once the first crop has been picked, hastens the formation of laterals and increases later crops on Brown Turkey and a few others.

In cold climates, where the trees must be protected heavily, cut back to live wood each spring.

Grapefruit

These bear somewhat earlier than oranges and more heavily. Also, they do not produce as many vigorous upright shoots, hence are not so tall. Otherwise, consider them the same as oranges.

Kumquat

Treat same as orange.

Lemon

Unlike oranges, lemons need fairly heavy pruning to keep them from putting out long straggly branches unable to carry the weight of the fruit they produce at their tips. Head young trees low and cut back laterals severely. Pinch back new growth several times during the season and remove all suckers and water sprouts.

In other words, try to produce a low, dense, twiggy growth. Four or five leaders per tree are often advisable. Determine the height, then remove all growth above it twice a year, as growth starts in spring and again in midsummer.

The Meyer lemon may be grown as a tub plant, dwarf, specimen shrub, or a hedge. Prune only for guidance.

Lime

Treat same as orange.

Limequat

Treat same as orange.

Loquat

This makes a neat, compact, round-headed tree. Thin out as necessary in fall if growth is too dense. Half of each flower cluster may also be removed to improve the size of the fruit, if desired.

Medlar

This is generally a shrub or small tree, related to the apple, pear, and quince. Treat somewhat like the pear and quince but keep it in tree form, like a miniature pear.

Mulberry

Small, rounded trees, these rarely need much pruning, except to remove dead, injured, or conflicting branches and for occasional shaping.

Nectarine

Treat same as peach.

Olive

In early stages train like an apple. However, the fruit is produced entirely on shoots of the previous year, and if they are not pruned, they tend to bear small, poor fruits and only in alternate years. Prune each winter, removing suckers, and thin out about forty per cent of the small, just-fruited branches to let in light and encourage new growth. Keep center open.

Orange

Oranges need little pruning once established. However, the first few years a little guidance helps. When planting, head back to three feet, leaving all laterals. The next few years keep the laterals growing upward. Remove suckers and strong spiny shoots. Then remove the lowest branches, a few each year until the trunk is clean two or two and a half feet from the ground. The other branches will arch and protect the trunk from sunburn.

After the fifth year remove dead and spindly growths but do not make big openings in the outer canopy of leaves. Trim top gently if needed to hold down height. If frostbitten, wait until extent of damage is evident, then cut back to the second live bud.

Pawpaw

These are generally considered a wild fruit and are rarely pruned. However, training into a small tree rather than a bushy thicket is preferred. Remove suckers and train as necessary.

Peach

The fruit is produced on the new wood of the year before. Thus, new fruiting wood must be produced each year. Train to an open center or a delayed open center. Once bearing starts keep the tree opened up moderately and prune as needed to keep the bearing

Two methods of pruning peach. Left, heading back each shoot. Right, removing whole sections with heading back of remainder

portions within reach. Also thin new growth to prevent overbearing
—the amateur rarely thins peaches enough. Remove all spindly
shoots and head back remaining ones to sturdy laterals or sound,
outward-pointing buds.

If the tree begins to get leggy, cut back hard on a few main laterals each year and in cold climates, if it is killed back noticeably,
use this opportunity to head the whole tree back. Each year look
for and remove winterkilled, broken, and crisscrossed branches. Remember that each piece of fruit needs fifty to seventy-five leaves
to support it properly.

Pear

Pears are usually trained according to the modified leader system,
somewhat like the apple, but with more scaffold branches left. Most
lateral growth is of the spur type and rarely gets too thick. The
fruits are borne on long-lived spurs on wood two or more years old.
In general, pears tend to be tight, upright growers. Thin out any
branches that are too narrow-angled to open up the tree. When
mature, the tree needs little beyond moderate thinning and a little
guidance. In fact, vigorous growth should not be stimulated by
heavy cutting, because it increases danger from the deadly fire
blight. Some varieties like Anjou, Bosc, Comice, and Hardy tend to
produce spurs only and need some spur-thinning to keep those remaining sufficiently vigorous and to ensure sufficient shoot growth.
All in all, pear trees can survive more neglect than practically any
fruit.

Persimmon

Train to a modified leader and, since the fruit is borne on current
growth, thin or head back as needed to keep new growth coming.
Do not cut too heavily or you will produce a mass of shoots and
little fruit. Some tend to overbear with accompanying danger of
limb breakage. Generally, they tend to prune themselves and many
small twigs die each year—remove them each spring.

In some areas it is also believed that a bark strangulation causes
fruit drop. If severe, the common practice is to cut several six- to
eight-inch slashes lengthwise in the bark of trunk and main
branches.

Plum

Japanese plums, which include most of the table plums (Abundance, Burbank, Satsuma, Santa Rosa, etc.), vary greatly in form. However, they are alike in bearing habits. They bear on short spurs lasting six to eight years with some additional bearing at the base of year-old shoots. Also, many tend to overbear and need severe thinning. For the most part, prune as for apricots, training the upright forms to spread and the spreading ones upright. Remove any signs of blackknot and eliminate weak crotches.

The European plums, which include the prunes, produce much longer "spurs"—in some cases a small branch. By comparison, they are much less likely to overbear. In any case, annually thin the older spurs and smaller branches to keep the center open and encourage new growth. Head back if too tall, and watch for injured branches.

Beach plums are one of the little-used American group. Usually they make a shrub or straggling tree four to ten feet high. The fruit is prized for jelly making. Pruning consists mostly of removing dead wood and a little moderate thinning of the older branches.

Pomegranate

Normally a large bushy shrub or small tree, it is best trained to a single stem. Remove all extra shoots at base. Head back and thin as necessary to keep vigorous fruiting wood at all times.

Quince

Because they are often subject to attack by borers and fire blight, it is safer to train them into bush form rather than tree form. After planting, head back to fifteen or eighteen inches and allow four or five scaffold branches to develop. Thereafter, pruning consists primarily of a little thinning to make spraying easier and to let air circulate. Prune off insect-injured tips and cankers, cutting back to laterals to stimulate new growth. Fruiting is at the tips of new shoots, so do not head back any more than necessary in any one year.

Tangelo and Tangerine

Treat same as orange.

XII . . . and Nut Trees

While many people believe that nut trees, being forest trees, never need pruning, they do need some guidance. However, it is not the kind of attention given fruit trees, but is more like that prescribed for ornamental or shade trees. Like them, they are almost always grown with a central leader. Since the crop (except for almonds) is one that falls to the ground and does not have to be picked, tall strong trees are generally preferred to low spreading ones that are more apt to break under a load of snow and ice or a heavy crop. Also, the higher a nut tree grows, the more crop-bearing surface it has.

As with shade trees, the height of the lowest branches is determined at planting or as soon after as possible. The trees are then pruned a little each year to establish the proper form and get the main branches started off right. Since, with few exceptions, nut trees bear on the growth of the previous year, they are always encouraged to produce a good crop of new wood, too. Usually, there is little need to push young trees into such growth, but as they get older the rate of growth declines and the older wood must be cut back to stimulate new shoots. Weak, damaged, shaded, crowded, or misplaced branches are always removed but cutting back to a stub is not recommended. Always cut to the parent branch or a live, preferably outward-facing bud. And do not cut back too hard—it removes too much crop-bearing wood. In general prune while dormant, just before growth starts in the spring. This usually shows up winter damage, too, if any has occurred.

Almond

Almonds are usually grown by the modified-leader or delayed open-center systems. Once the framework is established, about the third year, little pruning is necessary, with heading discontinued after the second pruning. Although some fruits are borne on the one-year wood, the bulk are produced on short spurs that last about five years.

After the tree has been bearing a few years, start renewing about a fifth of the spurs each year by removing some of the branches up to one and a half inches in diameter. This encourages new growth. If too heavy cutting is practiced, water sprouts result. They must not be allowed to remain, unless needed to replace broken branches.

Old trees may be rejuvenated by heading back the whole top to large, healthy laterals. In young trees that are too busy growing to flower, do the opposite—stop all pruning.

Beechnut

Beechnuts are mentioned frequently but it is reasonably safe to say that they are not truly cultivated in this country for the crop. Those that do bear are wild trees that need no care other than that given large shade trees.

Butternut

Treat same as walnut.

Chestnut

Ever since the coming of the chestnut blight, chestnut culture has been of little consequence in this country. However, the roots of our large native chestnut keep throwing up shoots, a few of which live long enough to fruit. Do not touch them except to remove blighted stems, cutting well below the injury.

Where the more resistant Oriental species and the hybrid forms are grown little pruning is done other than to guide the tree into building a good, strong scaffold and to remove infected portions. Protect all cuts with tree paint.

Coconut

As with other palms, do not top the trees. Old dying leaves may be removed as desired.

Filbert or Hazel

These are grown as shrubs or small trees. The nuts usually appear on the young shoots. If grown as a bush, frequent removal of a few of the oldest stems keeps the plants open and encourages vigorous new growth. Remove basal suckers by pulling them out of the ground rather than by cutting, in order to remove the adventitious buds at their bases.

When growing as a tree, use the central leader system and head the laterals back to keep new young branches coming.

Heartnut

Treat same as walnut.

Hickory

Train with a central leader and otherwise treat as you would a large shade tree.

Pecan

Treat the same as the hickories. On mature trees remove broken, diseased, or interfering limbs. Make cuts carefully and cover with tree paint.

Pine Nuts

These are produced on about four species of pine tree, usually wild. If necessary, prune only to correct shape of tree and to remove injured portions.

Pistacchio

This normally makes a small, open-headed tree, generally pruned for training only and to remove broken or otherwise injured portions.

Tung-Oil Nuts

Very little pruning is needed on established trees. Remove dead, weakened, or conflicting branches. Head newly planted tree back to eighteen inches after the buds have begun to swell. Then select those shoots that will make the best-placed branches. Train to prevent weak crotches and future damage from branches rising too close to each other.

Walnut

These large trees need very little pruning after they are sufficiently established. Remove all water sprouts and dead, diseased, or broken branches. To avoid spring bleeding, walnuts are often pruned in summer or fall.

Some growers recommend cutting young trees back to twelve to eighteen inches from the ground the first year and then allowing one shoot to grow. However, unless the root system has been badly damaged in the moving, there doesn't seem to be any gain in this. Perhaps there is even a setback. Simply train into a well-shaped central-leader or modified-leader tree, with the main branches at least two feet apart. On older trees, remove lower branches as they get in the way, always painting over the wounds. Central-leader trees yield better lumber when the trees are finally taken down.

XIII. Dwarfs and Special Forms

The basic principles that apply to large trees also apply to pruning dwarfs, but because of their smaller size and the fact that they are sometimes trained to special forms, some new twists must be introduced. And, in general, the pruning is a little more severe.

DWARF FRUITS

Unless otherwise trained, dwarf fruit trees differ from regular or standard trees in size only. Branching, budding, and blooming are characteristic of the variety. Dwarf trees do not bear smaller fruits. In fact, because of the greater ease with which they may be cared for, the fruits may even be larger.

Dwarfing of this sort is brought about by grafting the conventional top on dwarfing rootstocks. Apples may sometimes be found in a variety of sizes, being grafted on the so-called Malling Series of rootstocks. The one usually used on apples is Malling IX, which produces a tree five to seven feet high. Pears may be grafted upon quince roots and the others on various members of the plum group.

In pruning dwarf trees the direction in which the uppermost bud points is of increased importance, since everything is on such an intimate scale. Usually the growth is directed away from the center by cutting to outward-pointing buds, although occasionally if the tree is too spreading the reverse is done.

Here is another important point. Dwarf trees are usually more weakly rooted than full-sized ones. Hence, it is advisable to keep them staked at all times to avoid their being torn loose and toppled over in high winds. Also, it usually helps the restricted root systems to be a little more generous with food and water.

ESPALIERED ORNAMENTALS

Particularly on the West Coast the training of ornamental shrubs, and sometimes small trees on fences and walls, is gaining favor. Some of the more favored ones are pyracanthas, camellias, lantanas, fuchsias, and even magnolias. However, any plant that puts out buds readily and thrives under severe pruning is suitable. The form is usually the one that best suits the surrounding architecture; fans, horizontal cordons, and upright panels are the most common.

Most often, it is best to start with a young plant. Old ones rarely have branches in the right places and the severe cutting required is often difficult to heal or hide. It is best trained on a support of heavy wires, pipes, or wood in the desired form. The support is held four to eight inches away from the wall by brackets. This arrangement permits healthful air circulation around the plant, and removes the danger of decay in wooden buildings or structures.

Whether the new plant has a single leader or several at the time of planting is immaterial. The important thing is to follow the prescribed pattern. As soon as a leader or lateral reaches its limit in the given direction its end is cut. When new side shoots are forced out, they are either removed or trained in the new direction. If a light, airy growth or formal pattern is desired several trimmings a year may be necessary. If a fuller, more natural appearance is preferred, a once-a-year going over is sufficient. Plants that depend upon frequent renewal from the base cannot be expected to last many years without retraining new stems. Others, such as the magnolia, may easily outlive the trainer.

TRAINED EVERGREENS

The beauty of bark and limb of such trees as Scots pine is a highly desirable factor in modern landscaping. These evergreens may be trained in a variety of forms, particularly in an irregular Japanese fashion. To describe in detail how to do this is virtually impossible, for it depends upon the location, the size and shape of tree desired, and the nature of the tree to begin with. Judgment and taste are involved—as well as the principles outlined earlier in Chapter VI. In selecting training material, bear in mind that many needle-leaved evergreens do not break out buds readily from old wood.

The first step is to thin out the tree to gain a light, airy feeling. Then remove all dead or weak branches and those interfering with others. Now proceed with the real thinning of the remaining branches in order to produce your preferred design—an irregular pattern, horizontal tiers, or a spiral arrangement. Work carefully, remembering you can't put back what you have taken off.

Perhaps the easiest way to get an irregular effect is first to remove the terminal shoots and then such side ones as you think advisable. Thereafter, pinching back the "candles" or young shoots

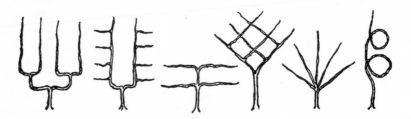

A few of the many shapes into which dwarf fruit trees have been trained

after new growth has started in spring is usually sufficient. All this tends to hold a tree down, so do not start such a program unless you plan to keep it up. As soon as you relax your care the tree will shoot up in natural fashion and the result will be a real monstrosity.

ESPALIERED TREES

With proper care, trees can be trained into almost any shape imaginable—cordons like grapes, flat triangles, pyramids, goblets, candelabra, fans, exclamation points, arches. However, unless you are willing to keep up such training indefinitely, it is better not to begin it. Usually it is easier to start with a shaped tree purchased from one of the few commercial sources, but for those who may want to train their own, we shall describe the formation of one of the simpler designs. The method is called the Lorette, after its French originator, and the form, the Double **U**.

Start with a one-year whip grafted upon a dwarfing root. The first spring cut it to within ten or twelve inches of the ground. From its uppermost bud will come a new terminal shoot. About mid-June (in the latitude of New York) cut this back to within less than half an inch of where it started. This should force out at least two new shoots at the same level and of about equal strength; if there are more than two, cut off the extras. Then tie the two shoots to a frame, rod, or other support to keep them horizontal. When they have achieved a length of twelve to fifteen inches turn the tips upward. (Bear in mind that in their final form all structural branches must be at least twelve inches apart.)

*A dwarf apple in bloom, trained into the Double-**U** form by the Lorette system*

The following spring and again in June, after the turned up branches have grown sufficiently, cut both back to twelve to fifteen inches above the bend and treat as you did the original shoot. This will produce four uprights to form the Double **U**. During these first few years, other shoots will start to grow. Cut all of these back almost, but not entirely, to the trunk or branch from which they came. In time this will turn them into fruiting spurs.

Now the tree has achieved its final form. To keep it at the desired height cut back the leading shoots each spring, leaving only one bud of the newest growth. During the summers continue removing all side shoots as before, cutting each back almost but not entirely to the point from which it started that season. If unwanted stem growth continues too vigorously, root prune every few years.

All other espalier forms may be made by following the same general principles.

In considering the location, remember that espaliers must have some sun and circulation of air. Southward-facing walls become too hot, especially for early-starting trees, such as peaches, which are also likely to be caught by late frosts. Eastern or western exposures are much better, although even northern ones can sometimes be used to produce late crops.

BONSAI

This is the Japanese method of training extremely dwarf trees. Since it involves several techniques other than pruning, such as supplying a meager diet, frequent replanting with pruning of the roots, tying or wiring of the branches, and so on, we cannot attempt to cover it here. To do a good job with this subject requires a whole book in itself.

XIV. Grapes: Table, Preserving, Wine

Cultivated grapes in this country are divided into three groups, each requiring somewhat different treatment. First, we have the grape of the East, the fox or bunch grape (*Vitus labrusca*), which includes varieties such as Concord, Worden, Delaware, Catawba, and Fredonia.

Next comes the muscadine grape (*V. rotundifolia*) of the South, including varieties such as Scuppernong, Flowers, James, and Thomas. Thirdly, we have the European grape grown on the West Coast. This includes such well-known varieties as Thompson Seedless, Muscat, Tokay, Malaga, Ribier, Zinfandel, Mission, and White Riesling. Each group will be taken up separately. Unless otherwise indicated, pruning is done during winter or early spring. If done late, just before growth commences, considerable bleeding occurs but it is not of earth-shaking importance.

FOX GRAPES

Because of their very wide distribution, we shall discuss these first. The best plants to set out are strong one- or two-year-olds. As usual, remove any dead or injured roots. After planting cut the best cane back to ten or eight buds and remove all other canes. When the new shoots reach a length of one inch all but the topmost one are rubbed off. If good growth results the first year, training can be begun. If not, cut back severely again and wait another year.

Kniffen System

Though there are many other pruning systems for grapes, this

one is in greatest favor. It is particularly well suited to such vigorous varieties as Concord and Fredonia, is productive, and requires
little summer tying. Tie the strong new shoot, mentioned above, to
the upper of two wires about three feet apart and cut it off just
above. If growth has been good, select four strong canes and train
them, two each on both the upper and the lower wires. On each
wire, lead one to the right and the other to the left. Cut them back to
five or six buds each and remove all other canes. If growth is weak,
delay starting the two upper canes until the following year, meantime cutting them back to one or two buds each.

On established vines cut off all wood grown the preceding year
except for one good strong shoot on each arm or cane, usually the
one nearest the trunk. Cut this back to ten to six buds, according to
the strength of the shoot. In a rough way this can be determined by
the diameter of the shoot. When its diameter gets down to less than
a quarter of an inch it is no longer sufficiently productive to bother
with. Repeat this each year. Tie the one-year portion to the wire,
letting the fruiting stems hang.

When the canes begin to age and the bearing parts are getting
farther and farther from the trunk, cut the canes back almost to the
trunk, one or two a season, and force out new shoots to take their
place. If the trunk appears to tire, cut it off and train a new one as
you did in the first place. It was once common to keep new spurs
coming for the replacement of canes but this is not necessary. If the
plant is so vigorous it can well afford to carry more than ten buds on
each cane, cut back to ten anyway but let an extra pair of canes
grow on the top wire.

The cardinal rule to remember in pruning grapes is: the fruit is
always borne on wood produced the same season which, in turn, is
borne on stems produced the year before. In other words, a year-
old piece of shoot produces buds in the fall. The next year it produces a shoot from each of these buds and later the same year at-
tempts to produce one to four bunches of grapes near the base of
each of these shoots.

High Renewal System

This system is better adapted to less vigorous growers such as
Catawba and Delaware. Here, in most cases, we have three wires

about twenty inches apart, but the trunk is stopped just below the bottom wire and two to six canes are trained upward on the wires. Frequent tying is necessary and unduly long shoots are cut back. Also, several renewal spurs—canes cut back to two buds—are continuously provided at the head of the trunk, for you don't leave the canes as permanent arms but replace them every year.

Fan System

Where winters are serious this system may be substituted. No trunk is used. The canes are trained upward, fanwise on the wires, and the head is kept close to ground level. This allows releasing the canes and letting them drop to the ground where they can be covered for the winter. Each year as many canes as the vine can support are saved and several more cut back into renewal spurs, for the canes are not permanent under this system either.

Arbor System

Most home gardeners prefer to grow their grapes on an arbor, since they are then ornamental as well as shade plants. Leave one trunk per vine if possible, although any number can be used if their canes are shortened correspondingly to keep them within the strength of the vine. Thus, the pattern is one you yourself set. Just remember where the fruits are borne and try each year to provide the proper number of buds on each of the new canes saved from the previous year's growth.

If the vine is old and neglected, you can cut it back severely in one year to thin it down to size or you can cut it back progressively harder each year until you get it where you want it.

SOUTHERN GRAPES

The muscadine produces its fruits in smaller bunches than the fox grapes. Usually, the plants are very vigorous. When setting them out, plant several inches deeper than in the nursery. Support them from the beginning, usually on a two-wire arrangement (three feet apart). Place the plants twenty feet apart.

Two to four arms are established somewhat as in the Kniffen system but the arms may be up to ten feet long. Then allow numerous two- or three-bud spurs on each. On the other hand, you can also develop a head at the top of a post and train the canes on overhead wires.

Muscadines may be pruned any time after the leaves fall, but for the most fruit, cut in February instead of before cold weather.

These are grown primarily in California and Arizona, for table use, raisins, and wine. Because of a different growth habit, training and pruning also differ. Their eventual use also governs pruning. Large, full bunches are grown for table use; quantity production for wine.

Left to right, *four-arm Kniffen system as used for eastern grapes and with slight modifications for southern ones, too.* Center, *head-spur system for European grapes.* Right, *cane system of training European grapes*

Unlike the other grapes named, the European varieties are often grafted on vigorous roots. Thus, suckers must be guarded against, particularly in the first few years, since the graft is usually kept on a level with the soil. The trunks of these grapes are heavier and thus need less support. Commercial growers usually use one of three systems: head spur, cordon spur, or cane. Home growers are likely to use arbors.

Head-Spur System

This is the easiest and cheapest and is used wherever possible for wine grapes. With judicious thinning, it can also be used for Tokays and Malagas for eating. After setting out, cut off all top growth except one cane. Cut this to two buds. Let shoots grow but not suckers. The second year, remove the weaker cane during the dormant season, cut the stronger back to two buds, and insert a strong six-foot stake next to the plant.

Again remove all growth except the leading shoot but don't remove side growths completely. Tie to the stake as needed and as soon as this shoot has grown eight inches or a foot above where you want the head, top it to encourage laterals and to thicken the trunk. The following winter pruning can be done from leaf-fall to bud-starting time. Then cut back to the bud next above the head, doing it in such a way that the bud is killed but the swelling remains to make tying easier. Take all weak laterals off and all strong ones from the bottom half of the trunk, shortening those left to three buds or less, according to the strength of their canes.

By the end of the next growing season there should be a trunk up to two inches thick, with four to eight strong canes. Save three to six of the best, well spaced and near the top. Cut them back to two to four buds. Thereafter, this rule may be followed for the number of buds to be left on the spurs: four buds, if thumb diameter; three if middle-finger diameter; two if little-finger diameter; one if pencil diameter. Later, if the arms get too long, replace with spurs closer to the trunk, such as those on the water sprouts.

Cane System

For fancy table grapes this is a better system, even though it requires two wires, one two to three feet high and another eighteen inches higher. It is especially useful with such varieties as Thompson Seedless, the first buds of which are not always fruitful.

Start training just as in the head spur method. Select two canes on either side of the trunk about level with the bottom wire, as well as two renewal spurs. Wind each cane or arm around the wire at least once to support the weight and tie well at the tip. If the vines are particularly husky, one or two more canes on each side may be permitted. Then tie the shoots to the wire above. This gives the leaves and developing fruit plenty of sun and keeps the fruit safely above splashings.

Arbor System

Simply train the vines with high heads and let them bear on either canes or spurs. However, since the trunks can suffer sun damage in the warm western climates, allow some short spurs to grow along their length to shade them with leaves.

Where the vines attempt to bear too heavily, it may be necessary to thin out the fruit. You can do this in either of two ways: by removing some of the flower clusters before they open, or by removing or thinning out oversized, undersized, or deformed clusters after the fruit has set. The first method is better for those varieties that set fruit poorly. It throws the strength into the clusters that are left. The second is especially useful on the varieties that tend to set too heavily. Sometimes the clusters are also thinned by removing side shoots or tips. This is a time-consuming operation and is practical only where the choicest table grapes are particularly desired, either in the home garden or commercial vineyard.

Grapes Under Glass

Though not a common practice in this country, especially high-quality grapes are sometimes produced in private greenhouses for show or table use. For this only the European varieties are used. The plants are spaced four feet apart and trained upward to about fifteen inches beneath the sloping glass roof.

Cut each back to two buds near the ground, save the strongest shoot, and tie it to the supporting wire. When it reaches the peak, pinch off the tip. In the fall, take it down, cut it back to a third of its length, lay it on the ground, and cover from the sun for the winter.

The following spring, again tie up the vine and let it run up to the top once more. Then pinch. Do not let the main stem fruit. Thin the laterals so that they stand a foot apart on either side. A few may be allowed to bear fruit but pinch off at the second eye beyond the cluster. Repeat the pinching, if necessary.

When the leaves fall, take down again. Shorten the terminal about half and cut the laterals back to a bud as close to the main stem as possible. Winter as before.

The third year, again pinch out when the main stem hits the top and do not allow it to fruit. Allow the laterals to bear. From now on pruning consists mostly of cutting the laterals back each year, close to the main stem, and rubbing off all but the strongest shoot when growth starts.

This is the spur system. Occasionally, the long cane system is used. Each year the cane is cut almost to the ground and a new stem trained in its place with the laterals pinched back beyond the clusters as above. This method can produce finer fruit but for most purposes the other method is better.

XV. Pruning Ornamental Vines

The pruning of vines is not too well understood and in general it is little practiced. Nevertheless, it is important for if it is not done, the vines become matted and choked with dead wood that prevents continued healthy growth and puts an unnecessary strain on the plants' supports.

NEW PLANTS

New vine plants should be set out in the same manner as any tree or shrub. Remove damaged roots or tops and cut back the top by a third to a half to compensate for the loss of feeder roots. (The cutting back need not be done if the plant is delivered growing in a container, or balled and burlapped.) Now shape and train as necessary to accommodate the support.

OVERGROWN ONES

Many vines, such as the matrimony vine and bittersweet, become too thick with age and need renovating. If in too bad shape, cut to the ground, select a few of the best shoots that then form, and train as a new vine. If less radical methods will suffice, start first by removing all the dead wood. Then thin out the oldest, toughest stems—to the ground, if possible. Lastly, remove whatever other growth seems advisable. In any case, do not just hack off, leaving the vine looking like a head of bobbed hair.

ROAD MAP TO PRUNING VINES—BY KINDS

Our discussion of vines, so far, has been rather sketchy, since there is little we can say that applies to all of them. However, we can now make up for that here by considering the important ones separately.

Akebia—**Five-leaved Akebia**

This is a hardy, almost evergreen vine that needs little care. It is not a heavy leafer and its growth is modest. If some shoots get too long, pinch off any time. Remove unwanted shoots preferably before growth starts in spring. One caution: place the shoots into their permanent positions early, since they get stiff as they age. Remove a few of the oldest stems occasionally to rejuvenate.

Aristolochia—**Dutchman's Pipe**

A rapid grower, reaching up to thirty feet, with large leaves. Twines around its supports. Head back as necessary to keep the base thick. Thin and remove dead shoots as needed. It will stand heavy cutting and comes back fast.

Bomarea—**Bomarea**

A plant of the amaryllis family, its twining growth is soft and somewhat succulent. Dies back to ground in frost areas. Cut off in late fall. It does not like to produce laterals and the flowers come at the tips. Do not pinch or head back.

Bougainvillea—**Bougainvillea**

Though considered a tender evergreen, the roots can stand considerable frost and will sprout vigorously. Thin and remove suckers. Stands any amount of cutting but severe cutting encourages stem growth at the expense of flowers in northern part of range. If frosted, do not cut back until new growth is well started.

In frost-free regions, it stands—and needs—much harder cutting and thinning, even twice a year without noticeable loss of bloom. One way to treat it is to thin and head back heavily in early spring, cutting all laterals back almost to the main stem. As soon as the tall, straight shoots finish flowering, cut tired stems.

Campsis—**Trumpet Vine**

For the warm-climate gardeners this group also includes such plants as *Clytostoma* (violet trumpet vine), *Doxantha* (cat's-claw),

Pandorea (Pandorea), *Phaedranthus* (Mexican phaedranthus), and *Tecomaria* (Cape honeysuckle). They are all strong-growing, clinging vines that need a fairly heavy support. Head back as needed to keep to support. Thin out and replace old stems when necessary. Keep after them, for if they get out of hand they are hard to control. If tender ones freeze back, cut off as needed when growth starts again. Remove suckers. Since they bloom on new wood, prune after flowering.

Celastrus—Bittersweet

There are two kinds, the Oriental and the native. Both are very vigorous, twining so tightly around young trees that, if not checked, they can kill them. Normally, the plants are either male or female, so both are needed. Thin or cut back as needed while dormant. Bittersweet prefers to grow upward rather than sideways. Both kinds bear their fruits pretty heavily on laterals, the Oriental back on the older parts, the native out on the tips where, of course, they show better. Keep this in mind when trimming. Both can be cut to the ground to renew. Remove suckers.

Cissus—Evergreen Grape

May need a little light heading back and trimming. If necessary, do it gently and frequently rather than all at once. Severely cut branches tend to die back.

Clematis—Clematis

These strikingly beautiful vines fall into two principal groups, those that bloom early on wood of the previous season and those that flower later on new growth. Study your plants, each one individually, determine which type it is, and time your pruning accordingly. Some are more rampant growers than others and need a little restraining but the clematis clan as a whole does not need severe cutting. If you have some that are more tender and freeze back, cut back to live wood after growth has started in spring.

Dolichos—Hyacinth Bean

Evergreen perennial vines in warm climates. Growth is fast and lush. If they tend to get out of hand, cut back. If really out of hand or frost-damaged cut to the ground in spring and guide the new growth.

Euonymus fortunei—**Wintercreeper**

When grown as a vine it seldom needs pruning other than a little snipping of tips to keep it from going where it is not wanted. When used as a ground cover it may need a little cutting to prevent its building up into pyramids. When trained as a shrub it needs guidance to shape it properly.

Gelsemium—**Carolina Jessamine**

An evergreen twiner that blooms in winter or early spring. Stands severe pruning, if desired. Do all pruning or thinning after flowering is over.

Hardenbergia—**Hardenbergia**

A shrubby half-climber. After blooming, cut off flower stems and weaker shoots. Gets leggy and thin without cutting back. Pinch during growing season, too.

Hedera—**English Ivy**

Attractive small-leaved evergreen vines climbing by rootlike holdfasts. Stand any amount of cutting back, any time. Remove unwanted growth.

Jasminum—**Jasmine**

Mostly evergreen shrubby or woody vines. Need little cutting besides thinning or tidying up. Flowers are produced on old wood, so do not cut heavily all at once. If too old and thick, remove a quarter of the oldest stems each year after blooming.

Lonicera—**Honeysuckle**

L. japonica is a very vigorous plant that not only rambles far but gets very thick. It stands heavy pruning. Therefore thin, remove suckers, and head back as needed any time after peak of bloom. Guide less vigorous sorts as needed.

Mandevilla—**Chilean Jasmine**

A deciduous summer bloomer that gets leggy. Cut to ground in the fall or cut and thin when dormant.

Panthenocissus—**Woodbine and Boston Ivy**

The first is a very vigorous vine that needs cutting back to keep it within bounds and to thicken it up.

Boston or Japanese Ivy is a fast-growing but more delicate vine for growing on masonry. Trim out where unwanted any time but if pulled off wall, cut back to firmly holding stem.

Passiflora—**Passion Flower**

Evergreen and vigorous. Not easy to thin out. If you have too much difficulty cut back to ground in spring after hard frosts are past.

Plumbago—**Leadwort**

A shrub or climber. Train either way. As shrub, cut back to force branching. When old, replace oldest stems with new ones, cutting to ground after blooming. If frozen, cut back. As a vine, thin out shoots, tie into place after flowering.

Polygonum—**Silver Lace-Vine**

Vigorous, twining, it blooms in late summer on new growth. Prune while dormant to keep in bounds. Tip pinching helps, too. May be cut to ground after flowering, if preferred.

Pueraria—**Kudzu Vine**

One of the fastest growing vines in warm areas. Though usually a ground cover, it will climb by twisting loosely. Pinch or cut back to thicken up.

Solanum—**Nightshade**

A thick, tangled grower, not easily thinned. If necessary, cut to ground in early spring.

Sollya—**Australian Bluebell Creeper**

Perhaps more often grown as a shrub but also makes a good little evergreen climber. Thin out to a few strong shoots and train after heavy frosts are past.

Streptosolen—**Streptosolen**

Remove spent shoots and clean up in spring. Remove winter damage. Stands heavy pruning. If thin, cut back to thicken.

Trachelospermum—**Confederate Jasmine**

A neat, evergreen, shrubby vine that seldom needs pruning. Train, thin, or head back as needed.

Wisteria—**Wisteria**

The best practice appears to be to let young plants cover most of the intended space before cutting. Then train somewhat as a grape: each fall cut back all new growths to two-bud spurs. Summer pinching also helps flowering but more important is horizontal training. When it can skyrocket upward it doesn't care to bloom. Root pruning is felt, by some, to aid reluctant bloomers.

In the warmer parts of California some people prefer to prune fairly heavily at the end of spring blooming. Often new shoots come that bloom again in summer. Head these back in fall.

Through the South, one often sees wisteria grown in tree form. Do this by selecting only the strongest stem. Trim off all side shoots continually. Top it when it reaches the desired height. Although it usually stays dwarf and blooms when it has nothing to climb on, cutting back to short spurs after the growing season is over appears to help.

XVI. The Badly Overgrown Garden

Until now we have been discussing pruning, in general, what and how to do it under ordinary conditions. But now let us assume that you have recently moved into an older home where trees and shrubs of all kinds are badly overgrown—as did the author when he came home from World War II. Just where do you start? How do you go about bringing order out of chaos? It's simple, if you tackle it slowly, step by step.

THE FIRST STEP

The first thing to do is to mow the lawn, if necessary, and to clean up any sticks, branches, and pieces of brush that may be on the ground. This will enable you to see first what you have and where your problems are: plume cypresses and other evergreens in front of the house are up to the second story windows; a hedge on one side and a row of lilacs on the other can droop and completely block the drive when it rains or snows; roses are badly overgrown; a row of mockoranges spreads fifteen to twenty feet and completely monopolizes one side yard; lilacs and vines completely hide the garage, etc.

Next, turn your attention to the drive. An unobstructed entry is essential. A hedge, like privet, is readily put back into shape. Take a pair of long-handled pruners or, if necessary, a key-hole saw to get into the small spaces and cut every stem down to within a foot, or so, of the ground. Regrowth will be rapid and you can easily train it into a neat hedge of any size you wish (see Chapter VII).

If you want a good hedge, full to the ground, don't let it grow to its full height at once. Increase its height in easy stages of, say, not more than six inches at a time, preferably less.

The lilacs on the other side of the drive should be cut back enough to get them out of the way. From there on it is simply a matter of rejuvenation, as outlined in the chapter on shrubs (V).

THE FRONT OF THE HOUSE

Next, turn your attention to what was once a well-behaved foundation planting. Trees like spruces, pines, and firs do not lend themselves to shortening. If they are too tall or too spreading they will have to come out. Don't try to dig them unless you are really ambitious. It is too much work. Merely saw them off at or just below the ground level. They are very unlikely to throw up repeated stump sprouts like broad-leaved trees.

Now you can turn your attention to the others. Trees like red cedars (junipers), arborvitae, yews, plume cypresses or retinosporas, to mention the most common ones, can be cut back by one-third and sometimes even one-half of their height. Then tie a small branch at the top into place to form a new leader for each tree and shape the trees back to their original outlines, as described in How to Handle Evergreens (VI).

From here on it doesn't matter what order you follow. My own choice would be to clean up the other side yard. Old shrubs can be rejuvenated but mockoranges such as those described earlier will still take up too much room in a narrow space. It is better to pull them out and replace them with something narrow like a rustic cedar fence or a row of space-saving columnar evergreens like red cedars or arborvitae. (Lombardy poplars are short-lived and lose their leaves in the fall, and their roots tend to plug sewers.) The cedars are best for hot, dryish places, the arborvitae for more sheltered or damper areas.

As for the overgrown shrubs you wish to remove, saw them off at any height that is convenient. Then dig a circle around each one to cut the roots. After that a stout rope, cable or chain fastened low and hitched to most cars will pull them out.

THE ROSES

These are preferably cut in early spring before growth starts but after all danger of freezing back is gone. If they are ever-bloomers but badly overgrown, simply cut them back to the normal height for spring pruning in your part of the country and proceed as outlined for regular pruning in Chapter VIII. Once-blooming shrub roses and climbers should be thinned out, removing the oldest stems first, and then trained as described in that chapter.

THE VINES

As with the roses, cut out all the way to the ground all the dead and tired, old stems. Remove their tops from the mass of tangled growth. Next cut out any tangles and overly-thick areas left. Finally shorten and shape the remaining portions to suit the location. If the vines happen to be wisterias or grapes, be sure to leave one trunk per plant and provide for the proper horizontal arms with their accompanying spurs (see Chapters XIV and XV).

PROBLEM TREES

Sometimes weed trees (like ailanthus in the neighborhood of many larger cities) grow up in unexpected and annoying places, for example close to houses or telephone wires. The author once had some that bumped into the attic (3rd floor) windows every time the wind blew.

The only recourse is to have them cut down piecemeal, or, if you are brave enough to do it yourself. In the latter case use a tall extension ladder or climb the tree and attach a long rope to each branch and piece of trunk that is likely to hit the house and damage it.

Then have someone pull on the rope, applying a moderately steady pressure so the portion will fall safely away from the house. Obviously, get yourself out of the way, too, before each portion comes loose and, remember, that they can sometimes kick back after they let go.

Sometimes, the stump grows out from under or right next to a porch where there isn't room enough to get in with a saw or axe. In such a case—and you will still want to get rid of it—there is one more way never mentioned, to my knowledge, before, but it works. Take a carpenter's brace and bit, set the rachet to turn the bit in the proper direction only and, describing what little arc you can with the handle, bore a series of adjoining and overlapping holes through the offending tree portion until you have severed it.

THE REST

This brings us to the remaining plants. Chapter VI fully describes what to do with broadleaved evergreens, whether they be rhododendrons, hollies, or tender exotics like dombeyas and podocarpus. Small fruits are covered in Chapter IX; tree fruits and nuts of all kinds in Chapters XI and XII. Ornamental and shade trees are covered in Chapter X.

In all cases remember the basics of pruning. First, clean out all dead wood, then take off diseased, dying, or broken portions. After that, remove any branches or parts that overcrowd or fight with others. Then thin out, shape, and train as the situation demands.

When should all this be done? The ideal season to prune each category is specified in the respective chapter. However, in emergencies you sometimes have to break the rules. In such cases do your cutting down, pruning back, thinning, or rejuvenation whenever you can. The trees, shrubs, or vines will usually survive, and further corrective measures can be taken later at the proper seasons.

One last comment. It usually pays to feed and water such heavily-pruned plants to help them overcome the shock of the operation. Feed shrubs and vines by placing fertilizer in holes dug with a crowbar, or apply liquid fertilizer with a root feeder. Foliar feeding—spraying the leaves with a dilute liquid fertilizer according to the manufacturer's directions—is also beneficial. However a few handfuls of a good tree-, rose-, or potato-fertilizer scattered over the surface of the soil under the branch tips in early spring and stirred in is usually sufficient.

Thereafter routine care should be practiced: weeding, spraying if necessary, removal of seed pods, and pruning, as described in other chapters of this book.

THE EXCEPTIONS

As a general rule, the broadleaved evergreens such as rhododendrons, camellias, andromeda, and Oregon holly grapes appear to need an acid soil. Throughout most of New England, the Southeast, and the Northwest this condition already exists, but in other parts of the country it may be necessary to acidify the soil as described in the next paragraph. Thereafter it is kept in balance by an occasional application of sulfur and by maintaining a two- to four-inch permanent mulch of oak leaves, acid peatmoss, pine straw, fir bark, or similar material. For the most part, these plants are shallow-rooted. Do not plant deeply and to avoid cutting the roots do not cultivate the soil.

If your soil is too limey for your plants, increase the acidity by mixing in powdered sulfur at the following poundage per one thousand square feet:

Your Soil pH	*The pH You Want*				
	7.0	*6.5*	*6.0*	*5.5*	*5.0*
8	20	30	40	55	70
7.5	15	20	35	50	65
7.0	0	15	20	35	50
6.5	0	0	15	20	35
6.0	0	0	0	15	15
5.5	0	0	0	0	5

Broad-leaved evergreens are also in greater danger of drying by winter sun and wind than deciduous shrubs, especially when grown beyond their usual range, in unusually windy locations, or where they get reflected heat from buildings. The safest practice is to grow any plants of questionable hardiness away from the sun, on the north side of the house rather than the south or east. A permanent mulch several inches deep should be maintained at all times and plenty of water given before the ground freezes. Then they should be given additional protection. The traditional, and unsightly, method has been to erect windbreaks of burlap or other material. A much better and more modern method is to spray the leaves at the onset of winter and again in January or February with a plastic coating such as Wilt-Pruf or Foli-Gard, available in good garden supply stores.

In the case of trees, water as needed and feed whenever the tree shows an unhealthy yellowish cast to the leaves or unnaturally short new growth. Make at least three rings of holes under the tree with a crowbar, at least 18 inches deep and 2 to 3 feet apart. One ring should be under the tips of the branches, one inside of that and one outside. There are rarely, if ever, any feeder roots next to the trunk. Into the holes place the fertilizer, water it, and then fill with soil. Some experts recommend a high-nitrogen fertilizer such as is used on lawns for shade trees and a more balanced one such as is sold for roses and root crops for flowering, fruit, and nut trees. Either one will help greatly. Apply it at the rate of one pound to each inch of trunk diameter measured four feet from the ground.

Another way to feed trees is with a root feeder that attaches to the end of your garden hose. Fertilizer cartridges placed into a chamber in the feeder are dissolved by the water and carried down to the roots.

In any case don't let the job of cleaning up the "overgrown" garden frighten you. Tackled in small pieces, step by step, the worst "jungle" can be tamed—and with much greater ease than you suspect.

XVII. Groundcovers

Groundcovers have become quite popular as alternatives to lawns in some areas. They are practical to hold steep banks, under trees, and in other shady places where grass does not grow readily, also in places where the pattern of a groundcover is wanted or the location is too rough to mow. However, good groundcovers are vigorous growers and occasionally need a little restraining or guidance.

There are two basic groups of groundcovers, the herbaceous or non-woody groundcovers and the woody ones. The first, being soft-stemmed, are easily restrained or otherwise handled. Among these are such perennials as ajuga, moss phlox (*Phlox subulata*), thyme, goutweed, wild ginger, English ivy, etc.

THE NON-WOODY TYPE

If they spread too far into a flower bed or lawn sever the offending portion from the rest of the planting with a shovel, spade, or edger, and pull or hoe these plants out. If they need thickening up or look too tired and weather-worn, they can be cut off with a sickle, scythe, rotary lawn mower, or brush cutter and given a feeding (three pounds per hundred square feet). They will soon be thick and lush again. These treatments may be given any time during the growing season, although early spring is better. Then the growth is more vigorous and the effects of any cutting soon lose their starkness.

WOODY GROUNDCOVERS

Being of a woody nature, these plants respond more slowly to treatments of any kind than the herbaceous ones. At the same time they are less likely to run rampant, and the effects of cutting or other treatment are likely to be more lasting.

In general, the best time of year to cut them back is just before new growth starts in the spring. Then a good vegetable fertilizer (rose and bulb fertilizers are essentially the same in most cases) applied at the rate of three to five pounds per hundred square feet and watered in will soon hide the scars of cutting. However, like taller shrubs, those that bloom early in the season can be cut immediately after blooming if the flowers are considered important.

There are three principal methods of cutting back woody groundcovers to thicken them up or to rejuvenate them with vigorous young growths. The first is running over them with a rotary mower set as high as possible. This applies principally to the not fully woody plants such as pachysandra, English ivies, and plants that grow in similar fashion.

Next come those which must be trimmed high but can still be given a general "hair-cut" with a scythe or sickle. These include climbing roses allowed to run over the ground, lowbush blueberries, and honeysuckle vines.

Finally, we come to those which must be cut back or pruned selectively like the junipers, bearberries, and cotoneasters. These should be cut back like any tree or shrub to just above a side branch or start of one. Any portions, herbaceous or woody, that are spreading beyond the limits set aside for them may be cut off at any time in nearly all cases. (See Chapter V and VI).

Vines, as a group, may be cut anywhere along the canes so long as the cut is made just above a leaf node or joint.

ROAD MAP TO PRUNING GROUNDCOVERS

The comments above are somewhat brief but the following list offers supplemental information on specific plants. Figures refer to height: Care to vertical control is given first, lateral second.

Acaena — **Acaena**
KIND: Semi-evergreen perennial. Slow to fast spreader (9″).
CARE: Shear or prune as situation calls for.

Aegopodium — **Goutweed**
KIND: Spreading herbaceous perennial (6-10″).
CARE: Shear or mow top to thicken, if thin. Weed sides.

Ajuga — **Bugle**
KIND: Flowering, herbaceous perennial (4-6″).
CARE: Shearing unnecessary. Sever and weed out to hold within bounds.

Akebia — **Akebia**
KIND: Dainty vine. Fast growing. Deciduous.
CARE: Cut wherever needed.

Anthemis — **Chamomile**
KIND: Perennial. Scented. Moderate spreader. Sun, half-sun.
CARE: No problem. Stands a rare mowing.

Arctostaphylos — **Bearberry**
KIND: Woody creeper (4-6″). Slow grower for poor soil.
CARE: Use scythe or shear to thicken. Cut above nodes to restrain.

Aronia — **Chokeberry**
KIND: Deciduous, flowering shrub (12-30″).
CARE: Not a fast grower. Prune like any other shrub.

Asarun — **Wild Ginger**
KIND: Herbaceous perennial (6″). Moderate spreader.
CARE: Shearing not necessary. Sever and weed to hold within bounds.

Asperula — **Sweet Woodruff**
KIND: Fragrant, spreading perennial (8″).
CARE: Pull out as necessary.

Calluna — **Heather**
KIND: Thick-growing, evergreen flowering shrub (6-24″).
CARE: Shear when thin and leggy. Cut back almost anywhere to restrain.

Campsis — **Trumpet Vine**
KIND: Large-leaved, deciduous, flowering vine. Rapid grower.
CARE: No height problem. Cut wherever necessary.

Carisia (Dwarf) — **Natal Plum**
KIND: Small evergreen shrub for South. Slowish grower.
CARE: Not particularly spreading but stands shearing.

Ceanothus — **Prostrate Ceanothus**
KIND: Generally deciduous shrubs. Prostrate. Blue flowers. Mild areas.
CARE: Little. Moderate spreader. Usual pruning. Mild Areas.

Celastrus — **Bittersweet**
KIND: Rampant, twining vine. Berry-bearing.
CARE: No height problem, if can't climb. Cut wherever necessary.

Cerastium — **Snow-in-Summer**
KIND: Grayish. White flowers. June (3-6").
CARE: Weed out as necessary.

Convolvulus — **Mauritanian Bindweed**
KIND: Prostrate perennial. Blue-violet flowers.
CARE: Soft. Cut back with grass shears as needed.

Cotoneaster — **Rockspray**
KIND: Fine-leaved, angular shrub (12-24").
CARE: Prune like any shrub to thicken or restrain lateral growth.

Daphne cneorum — **Garland Flower**
KIND: Low, spreading, evergreen shrub. Rosy flowers (6-8").
CARE: Little. Cut back only when necessary.

Empetrum — **Crowberry**
KIND: Very low, creeping, fruiting, almost-needled evergreen shrub (2-5").
CARE: Restrain side growths, if necessary.

Epimedium — **Epimedium**
KIND: Flowering herbaceous perennial. Upright (8-12").
CARE: Weed out as needed.

Erica — **Heath**
KIND: Thick-growing evergreen, flowering shrub (6-12").
CARE: Shear when thin and leggy. Cut back almost anywhere to restrain.

Euonymus — **Wintercreeper**
KIND: Viney, evergreen shrub (6"). Fair spreader.
CARE: Rarely needs thickening. Cut anywhere to restrain.

Festuca — **Blue Fescue**
KIND: Fine grass in clumps (6").
CARE: Slow-spreader. Cut to ground in spring. Little cutting needed, if ever, for restraint.

Forsythia — **Arnold Dwarf** (var.)
KIND: Non-flowering, trailing shrub. Deciduous (24-30").
CARE: Cut old plants to base to rejuvenate. Cut at any node for guidance.

Galax — **Galax**
KIND: Herbaceous, flowering, evergreen perennial (6").
CARE: Scythe or mow to rejuvenate. Weed to restrain.

Gaylussacia — **Box Huckleberry**
KIND: Evergreen shrub, not overly spreading (18").
CARE: Scythe or mow, if needed. Prune in conventional manner.

Gaultheria shallon — **Salal**
KIND: Long, creeping shrub.
CARE: Usual pruning as needed.

Gazania — **Gazania**
KIND: Perennial in mild climate.
CARE: Rapid spreader. Cut back or grub out as needed.

Genista, Prostrate — **Creeping Broom**
KIND: Long, creeping shrub.
CARE: Usual pruning as needed.

Hedera — **English Ivy**
KIND: Woody, evergreen vine (6″).
CARE: Scythe or mow to rejuvenate or thicken. Cut at any joint to guide.

Hypericum calycinum —
St. Johnswort
KIND: Evergreen shrub. Spreads by stolons. Yellow flowers (12″). For sun or shade.
CARE: Scythe tops to thicken. Grub out if spreads.

Iberis — **Hardy Candytuft**
KIND: Semi-woody perennial. Showy, white-flowered (6-12″).
CARE: Shear off, if tired looking or straggly.

Juniperus — **Juniper**
KIND: Woody, needle-leaved evergreen (6-24″).
CARE: Cut back to any joint or crotch.

Lantana — **Trailing Lantana**
KIND: Rapid-spreading, vining shrub.
CARE: Prune to train as needed.

Leiophyllum — **Prostrate Sand Myrtle**
KIND: Low, creeping, evergreen shrub.
CARE: Slow growing. Little pruning.

Liriope — **Lilyturf**
KIND: Grassy and perennial. Dependable in warm climate (8-10″).
CARE: Resists unfavorable quarters. Grub out, if spreads.

Lonicera — **Honeysuckle**
KIND: Deciduous or semi-evergreen, woody vine.
CARE: Scythe or mow to rejuvenate or thicken. Cut whenever necessary.

Mahonia repens — **Creeping Hollygrape**
KIND: Creeping, evergreen shrub. Spreads by stolons. Mild climate (12″).
CARE: Little. Prune to prevent undue spread.

Mesembryanthemum — **Iceplant**
KIND: Evergreen and perennial in warm climates (6-18″).
CARE: Adapted to hot, dry places without care. Remove unwanted plants.

Ophiopogon — **Dwarf Lilyturf**
KIND: Grassy and perennial. Survives on adversity (6″).
CARE: Takes care of itself in south. Grub out, if spreads.

Pachistima — **Pachistima**
KIND: Small deciduous shrub. Sun or shade (12″).
CARE: Shear carefully after flowering.

Pachysandra — **Japanese Spurge**
KIND: Evergreen, semi-woody plants (6″).
CARE: Scythe or mow to keep thick. Weed out unwanted plants.

Phlox subulata — **Moss Phlox**
KIND: Creeping, spreading, showy-flowered perennial (6″).
CARE: Always thick. Weed out unwanted plants.

Polygonum reynoutria — **Knotweed**
KIND: Herbaceous, fast spreading (6-10″).
CARE: Hoe out unwanted plants.

Potentilla tridentata — **Wineleaf Cinquefoil**
KIND: Low, spreading, cold-resistant (2-6″).
CARE: No care beyond rare feeding, pulling a few plants.

Pyracantha — **Firethorn**
KIND: Vigorous woody shrub. Deciduous.
CARE: Must be kept low by judicious but severe pruning.

Rosa — **Climbing Roses**
KIND: Vigorous, deciduous, flowering, woody trailers (6-12″).
CARE: Scythe occasionally to rejuvenate. Cut to any node to restrain.

Rosmarinus Prostrate — **Creeping Rosemary**
KIND: Fragrant, evergreen subshrub especially for mild climates.
CARE: Prune as needed to guide.

Santolina — **Lavender Cotton**
KIND: Rapid-growing, gray subshrub (20″).
CARE: Guide and restrain by shearing or pruning.

Sarcococca — **Sarcococca**
KIND: Evergreen shrub in warmer states (12-24″).
CARE: Stands shearing. Not too spreading.

Saxifraga sarmentosa — **Strawberry Geranium**
KIND: Dainty, trailing vine for warm areas.
CARE: Pull out unwanted plants.

Sedum — **Sedums**
KIND: Small, succulent, flowering perennial (4-12″).
CARE: Thickening ineffective. Weed out as needed.

Sempervivum — **Hen and chickens**
KIND: Small, hardy perennial (3-6″).
CARE: Merely pull out few plants that spread.

Taxus — **Yew**
KIND: Needle-evergreen. Heights, various.
CARE: Stands heavy pruning or shearing.

Teucrium — **Germander**
KIND: Low herb or subshrub.
CARE: Well-behaved. Shear or prune for shape and cover.

Thymus — **Thyme**
KIND: Ground-hugging, dainty, flowering perennial (2-5″).
CARE: Feed to thicken. Pull or hoe unwanted plants.

Trachelospermum — **Confederate Jasmine**
KIND: Woody, evergreen vine. Fragrant, white flowers.
CARE: Needs little guidance or restraining.

Vaccinium misc. sp. — **Dwarf Blueberries**
KIND: Low, deciduous, fruiting shrub (6-15").
CARE: Scythe or mow as needed. Hoe out unwanted plants.

Vaccinium vitis idea — **Mountain Cranberry**
KIND: Tiny, broad-leaved evergreen (3-7").
CARE: Needs sour soil and moisture. Hoe unwanted plants.

Vitis — **Grapes**
KIND: Very vigorous trailers, non-evergreen.
CARE: Scythe to ground occasionally and feed. Cut to any node.

Verbena — **Verbena**
KIND: Usually treated as repeating annual. Colorful blooms (12").
CARE: No pruning needed. Hoe out if spreads.

Vinca — **Myrtle**
KIND: Dainty, fast growing, evergreen trailer (4").
CARE: Scythe or mow to thicken. Cut anywhere to restrain.

Xanthorhiza — **Yellowroot**
KIND: Upright deciduous shrub (18-24").
CARE: Scythe or mow to thicken. Grub out unnecessary plants.

XVIII. Tree Farming

Tree farming has grown by leaps and bounds in the United States in the last few years and promises to grow even more in the years to come. Hence, a brief resume of the highlights of this important operation are in order.

For our purposes, there are three principal types of tree farming: (1) the raising of seedling trees to set out elsewhere; (2) farming for the harvesting of wood; (3) the most important from our standpoint, the raising of Christmas trees.

SEEDLING TREES

The successful culture of tree seedlings demands some attention. They cannot thrive where there is neglect. First the seed is sown in rows six inches apart or broadcast in bands in a frame. Then it is watered when necessary, shaded, weeded, thinned, and protected from rodents. In thinning, twenty to twenty-five seedlings are permitted per foot of row if they are to be sold or used when two years old. This is done in early spring before the second season of growth begins.

Also at the end of the first growing season they should be root pruned as soon as they are dormant. In comparatively small plantings a long, thin knife is pulled through the soil at a 45° angle half way between the rows or three inches from the plants on either side. The knife should penetrate eight or nine inches beneath the surface at the deepest point. Larger plantings can be so treated with a sharp spade and still larger ones with a tractor-pulled knife.

At the end of the second season of growth seedlings are frequently dug up and again root-pruned, whether they are to be replanted or disposed of elsewhere. In this case, however, the roots are chopped to a standard four or five inches with a machete or other heavy knife on a block of wood.

IN WOOD PRODUCTION

When, how, and how much to cut are matters of common sense and depend on one's needs and the situation at hand.

Young trees need light and air to grow. Cut down to the ground any that are weak, damaged, or interfering with or shading others of the same size. Later when they get larger one rule of thumb is that evergreens do best when spaced fourteen feet apart when the diameter measures six to ten inches at breast height (four feet).

Removing the branches from the bottom up produces good, clear, knot-free lumber. In such cases the trees are first pruned when three to four inches in diameter; the best time is early spring before growth starts. Use a sharp saw or long-handled shears. In no case chop off the branches—healing is poor, rot may gain entry, and you may have holes in the subsequent lumber.

Frequently, trees are first pruned (especially in the case of evergreens) when they have reached a diameter of four to six inches at breast height. Never remove more than one-third of the active green branches at a time and always work from the bottom up.

After the trees have grown larger, additional pruning may be done. One practice is to clean the trunks up to about sixteen feet (or two eight-foot logs). Pruning beyond that becomes less practical for it involves ladder work.

CHRISTMAS TREE FARMING

Of the three types of tree operation, this one will probably be of interest to the largest percentage of readers, whether their tree plantation is home- or commercial-sized.

When should one commence such training? Generally, when the

trees are two to two-and-one-half feet tall, or the third to fourth year after planting for pines and one year later for firs and spruces. (Of course, species vary and so do growing conditions, but these figures strike a reasonably good average).

This first shearing should include removing extra stems and deformities and cutting back the terminal and lateral shoots. Then the bottom whorl of branches should be removed to produce a "handle" for later convenience.

A second shearing should take place a year or so later. Again the terminal and the lateral shoots should be cut back. Follow with the same treatment a year later.

In the case of pines a fourth shearing is frequently done in the sixth year. Special attention is paid to developing an attractive-length leader and excessive side growth is curtailed. In the seventh and eighth years it is best to let the tree grow out a bit. Only extreme growth is checked and the tree is harvested at the end of the seventh or eighth year and with a height of five to seven feet.

Three shearings are usually enough for spruces and firs before they are allowed to grow out. They are harvested in the eleventh to twelfth years, also at the height of five to seven feet.

THE BEST TIME TO SHEAR

What time of year is best for shearing? Do it in late spring to early summer, generally June 1 to August 10 according to one's location—earlier in the South and later in the North. This allows the candles or new growth to practically complete its lengthwise increase but it is still soft and succulent. Shearing too early results in a too-profuse bud set and often an irregular growth. Too late a shearing produces a shortage of buds, slow development of those present, and frequently dead stubs.

How is this shearing done? Using a knife, sickle, hedge- or pruning shears, or a machete, start with the central leader. Decapitate it at a height of twelve to fourteen inches on pines. Make the top whorl of laterals three to five inches shorter. Then proceed to the other laterals. Finally shorten any over-long branches to the nearest practical branchlet.

Do not make the growth too tight so the tree is a blob, without airiness and grace. Also, all cuts should be made at a 45° angle, if possible. It looks better and seems to discourage the formation of multiple buds.

These instructions apply especially to white and Scotch pines, which are relatively fast growers. Norway (red) and Austrian pines are slower growing. Don't cut back as far proportionately. Sometimes just nipping the tips is enough.

With spruces and firs cut the leader to eight to twelve inches, making the cut not over a half-inch above a good-looking, individual bud (not a cluster). Then, similarly, shape the rest of the tree.

While these instructions about cutting the terminal or lead shoot appear to be contradicting the instructions not to do so earlier in the book, this is done intentionally. Cutting the terminal shoot on these trees is clearly a dangerous practice for the neophyte and one that should definitely be discouraged. However, if one is experienced and interested enough to go into the raising of high-grade Christmas trees, it is assumed that he is sufficiently proficient to take this risk. In any case, one must never forget that the period when these terminals can be cut with safety is very short. Generally, it lasts only about ten days.

One alternative also exists. In some areas there is still a tendency to harvest the trees so that a branch or two remains on the trunk. The idea is that at least one will turn upward and the strong root system still remaining can turn this into a new top more quickly than when starting with seedlings. If you wish to try this, do so on a purely experimental basis. Then you are less likely to be disappointed if you do not handle the trees correctly. If things turn out favorably, you are ahead of the game.

Index